Dedication

This book is dedicated to the German and Austrian survivors and their families, many of whom died at the hands of the Nazis. We also wish to honor those brave individuals whose generosity and kindness often made the difference between life and death for those in peril.

Acknowledgments

This project originally began as a way of commemorating the 60th anniversary of *Kristallnacht*. Present and former reporters from the *Democrat & Chronicle* as well as other writers graciously agreed to interview and write articles on German and Austrian survivors now living in the Rochester area. We are grateful to Doug Mandelaro for spearheading this initiative and to Dr. Michael Dobkowski for consulting with us. We thank all those who donated their time and expertise to this project.

We are extremely indebted to the survivors who gave so willingly of their time, often agreeing to long hours of interviews and sharing painful memories with us. Some profiled here gave us their memoirs, which we have adapted for this book. All shared as well their cherished family photographs and documents.

We wish to thank others who made this book possible, notably Susan Huyser, whose imaginative and bold designs brought the subject matter to life, and Deborah Harkins, who helped fine-tune the manuscript with loving care. We thank Chris Sims of the U.S. Holocaust Memorial Museum for his assistance in photo research. We are especially grateful to the BIL Charitable Trust for providing the editorial team and funds needed to produce this book and guiding it from inception to conclusion.

Finally, we thank the Board of Directors of the Jewish Community Federation and the members of the Steering Committee of the Center for Holocaust Awareness and Information (CHAI) for their encouragement and support. We thank the members of the Consortium of Holocaust Educators headed by Dr. Karen Shawn for their insights and support of this project from its inception. And we thank our families for their support and help in realizing this book.

Contents

Perilous Journeys

Personal Stories of
German and Austrian Jews
Who Escaped the Nazis

Creative Director and Editor: Barbara Lovenheim

Editor: Barbara Appelbaum

Publisher: The Center for Holocaust Awareness and Information (CHAI)
of the Jewish Community Federation of Greater Rochester, New York

ISBN 0-9710686-0-7

Produced by the BIL Charitable Trust
315 East 65th Street, NY, NY 10021
E-mail: BLovenh214@aol.com

Published in the United States of America
2001 by the Jewish Community Federation
of Greater Rochester, New York
441 East Avenue, Rochester, NY 14607

For information contact
Barbara Appelbaum, Director CHAI
Telephone: 1 716 461-0490
E-mail: bappelbaum@jewishrochester.org

To order books call
Book Masters
Telephone: 1 800 247-6553

Shattered Lives: The Courage to Remember

The stories you are about to read are based on the memories of a special group of German and Austrian survivors who now live in Rochester, New York. All these individuals grew up under Nazism, and they remember watching as their parents were stripped of their homes, their possessions, their businesses, and their careers by the German government. After the *Kristallnacht* pogrom in November 1938, most Jewish families sought refuge in the U.S., England, or Palestine. But only a few were able to obtain visas to these countries. Other families had to seek refuge in distant lands they had only read of in travel books. They fled to any country that would accept them—countries like China, Africa, Cyprus, and India—where they didn't know the language or the customs. Often, they arrived penniless. One family—the Arndts—who wouldn't go to these distant lands, eventually had to hide in Berlin, entrusting their lives to non-Jewish friends.

In the early years of Nazism, parents tried to shelter their children as best they could, but they were powerless to prevent schoolmates from snubbing and insulting their children because they were Jewish. All these children had a hard time making sense of a world suddenly turned topsy-turvy. Nathan Taylor was hurt and bewildered when all his classmates received Hitler Youth uniforms and were told to march in the schoolyard. From the taunts of a classmate Evie Jacobson learned, for the first time, that her father was Jewish. Kurt Weinbach was only a youngster when his parents made the agonizing decision to uproot the family and face the uncertainties of life in China.

Some survivors, such as Bill Braun, Rosemarie Molser, and Hermann Goldfarb, had to leave their families and travel alone to safe havens when they were only teenagers. Others, like Lily Haber, married hastily and bore children in harsh environments. The lives of everyone were dramatically changed.

Some of the survivors profiled here have never told their full stories to the public. Others have talked to students through our Center's *Survivors in the Classroom Project*, a project that reaches over 9,000 students a year, giving students a vivid sense of how difficult it was surviving in Nazi Germany and Austria. We are extremely pleased that students will now be able to read the stories of these survivors in conjunction with their classroom visits.

But we believe that these stories, photographs, and documents have a wider audience. Whether we are young or old, we can all learn important lessons from these remarkable individuals, stories about enormous resilience in extraordinary circumstances, of resourcefulness and courage in the face of unimaginable odds, of hope and faith in family and friends, whose courageous actions often made the difference between life and death. We hope that these profiles endure as a source of inspiration and strength for succeeding generations, and we are extremely proud to be publishing them.

Barbara Appelbaum, Director, Center for Holocaust Awareness and Information (CHAI)

The Rising

O N NOVEMBER 9, 1918, KAISER WILHELM II—the monarch who had led Germany into a brutal world war—abdicated. One of the deadliest wars in European history was over. But the resulting peace and the harsh terms of the Treaty of Versailles crushed Germany's economy and its spirit. Germans had to pay huge reparations to the Allied victors—reparations they couldn't afford. They were forced to disarm completely. And the new, democratic Weimar Republic, led by General von Hindenburg, was shaky at best, founded on a hopelessly idealistic and impractical constitution.

Instead of reducing tensions in the country, the new constitution exacerbated the strife between right-wing imperialists—who wanted a return to a monarchy—and left-wing socialists and Communists—who wanted a democratic government. Nasty street brawls broke out between right-wing officers and laborers.

The German mark plunged in value, setting off the worst inflation in German history. American banks began lending money to the Germans and the economy gradually started to improve. Then, in the fall of 1929, the American stock market collapsed, setting off a worldwide depression. In Germany, factory work halted. Six million people were unemployed. Despair was pervasive.

In this environment the National Socialist (Nazi) party began to flourish. Led by an Austrian zealot named Adolf Hitler, this right-wing party was composed of malcontents, anarchists, and racists who hated the Jews and the Bolsheviks. The Nazis aimed to demolish democracy, expand Germany's boundaries, and set up a state of pure-blooded "Aryans"—Germans without any trace of Jewish blood.

Hitler, a genius at manipulating crowds, managed to mesmerize Germans with his rhetoric, blaming the Jews and the Communists for Germany's defeat in World War I. Despite working-class opposition, the Nazis won 13.5 million votes in the 1932 elections, becoming the largest party in Germany.

Opposite page: Adolf Hitler and Heinrich Himmler reviewing SS troops during Reich Party Day ceremonies, Nuremberg, Germany, September 1938.

Storm

Hindenburg, the president of Germany, lost all power to pass effective laws or curb the street violence that Hitler had purposely engineered to paralyze the existing government. Finally caving in to pressure from conservatives and nationalists who were helpless at maintaining order, Hindenburg named Hitler Chancellor. Eventually, he reasoned, Hitler would turn to the conservatives for guidance. Laborers, however, were horrified: When reports of the appointment leaked out, 100,000 workers gathered to protest in the Lustgarten, a large public park in Berlin.

The protest had no effect. On January 30, 1933, Hitler went to the Reichstag (the parliament building) to make his first public appearance as Chancellor. On February 27 the Reichstag burned in a mysterious fire that the Nazis blamed on the Communists and used as a pretext to declare a state of emergency. Despite the coup, the Nazis won only 44 percent of the popular vote in the March 5 elections. To secure his power, Hitler finessed the passage of an "Enabling Act" that gave him dictatorial powers. He used it to abolish the Weimar Republic and its parliamentary democracy.

The Nazi nightmare was about to begin.

The Jews Are to Blame

WHEN HITLER CAME INTO POWER IN 1933, there were some 525,000 Jews living in Germany—less than 1 percent of the entire population. About a fifth of these Jews were recent émigrés from Eastern Europe, most of whom worked as peddlers, factory laborers, and artisans. But the overwhelming majority of the country's Jews—80 percent—were native-born Germans who belonged overwhelmingly to the middle class. They were also fiercely nationalistic. Sixteen percent had fought bravely in World War I, and many had earned the Iron Cross for distinguished service.

Most Jews lived in large cities—about 150,000 lived in Berlin—and many were prominent in business, commerce, newspapers, science, medicine, law, and the arts. Erich Arndt's father and Gerry Glaser's father were respected doctors in Berlin, each with a large Jewish and non-Jewish clientele. Rosemarie Molser's father was an outstanding lawyer. All three men had served with distinction in World War I. Warren Heilbronner's grandfather and his brother owned a large textile company in Stuttgart.

In her book *Between Dignity and Despair: Jewish Life in Nazi Germany*, Marion Kaplan discusses Jewish religious observance. She points out that only 10 percent of Germany's Jews were Orthodox. Most Jews were liberal in their practice of Judaism, similar in observance to Conservative Jews in today's world. These German Jews belonged to synagogues, celebrated bar mitzvahs with great pride, and observed the major Jewish holidays. Most interacted easily with their non-Jewish neighbors and business associates. Assimilation was, in fact, so pervasive that by 1927, a quarter of all Jewish men and 16 percent of Jewish women were marrying outside their religion.

Despite the Jews' apparent social acceptance, there was in Germany an underlying antisemitism that Hitler brought to the surface and manipulated for his own purposes. Hitler's goal was to use propaganda, economic impoverishment, and forced emigration to isolate Jews, who had gradually assimilated into German economic, political, and social life.

Appealing to his countrymen's vanity, greed, and fears, Hitler blamed the Jews for Germany's loss of world power and its turbulent economy. Claiming that Jews and Bolsheviks alike were inciting a conspiracy to control the world, he organized bands of citizens into a private army known variously as SA men, storm troopers, and Brownshirts and sent them to attack Jewish-owned businesses and shops. At the same time, *Der Stürmer*, a rabidly antisemitic tabloid, fanned the flames, portraying Jews as evil-looking perverts and criminals. Gypsies, homosexuals, the

Top, left to right: Front page of the Nazi publication *Der Stürmer*, with an antisemitic caricature depicting the Jew as the hater of all non-Jews. Three Jewish businessmen are forced to march down Bruel Strasse, a main street in Leipzig, carrying signs that read "Don't buy from Jews. Shop in German businesses!" 1935.

OCTOBER 28, 1938	17,000 Polish-born German Jews expelled to Polish border.
NOVEMBER 7, 1938	Herschel Grynszpan shoots Ernest vom Rath, minor German official, in Paris.
NOVEMBER 9-10, 1938	*Kristallnacht:* 1,000 synagogues burned; 7,000 Jewish shops looted; 30,000 Jewish men arrested.
NOVEMBER 15, 1938	Jewish children can no longer attend German public schools.
MAY 27, 1939	Cuba refuses to admit 900 German Jewish refugees from the ship St. Louis; U.S. also rejects them.
SEPTEMBER 1, 1939	Germany invades Poland; two days later, France and Great Britain declare war on Germany.
APRIL 9, 1940	Germany invades Denmark and Norway.
MAY 10, 1940	Germany invades Belgium, France, Holland, and Luxembourg.

mentally retarded, and the physically handicapped were also targeted for attack by the Nazis.

Despite this active propagandizing, many Germans did not heed Hitler's attacks on Jews right away. A month after Hitler took power—April 1, 1933—Hitler ordered a boycott of all Jewish-owned businesses and professional offices. Few Germans obeyed the boycott. Some were openly defiant, passing through police barricades. Because many Germans at first did not support the boycott and ignored Hitler's vicious antisemitic tirades, most German Jews were not alarmed enough to leave their beloved country.

But the Nazis continued to churn their gospel, appealing often to youngsters in Hitler Youth groups. On May 11, thousands of students gathered in a plaza opposite the University of Berlin and set fire to hundred of books considered hostile to the government.

"The soul of the German people can again express itself," said Joseph Goebbels, Hitler's chief propagandist, watching the works of Thomas Mann, André Gide, Jack London, and other famous authors burn to ashes. "These flames not only illuminate the final end of an old era; they also light up the new."

The Exodus Begins

ALTHOUGH MOST GERMANS BELIEVED that Hitler would be overthrown, emigration began as soon as he took power. In 1933, between 60,000 and 65,000 Germans fled the country; 37,000 were Jewish. The majority went to neighboring countries—France, Holland, Denmark, and Belgium. Others sought haven in England, South America, Canada, and the U.S.

Jews continued leaving Germany in the next years, but many others remained, confident that Hitler would soon be ousted. Erich Arndt's father, for example, did not think his countrymen would tolerate Hitler for long. Tied to their culture and language, such Jews were willing to endure the hardships of the known rather than risk the unknown. Others, like Ellen Arndt's mother, Charlotte, were taking care of their elderly parents and refused to leave them. They and others coped with displays of antisemitism as Jews had coped with prejudice for centuries: by downplaying it and waiting it out, living as best they could and trusting that life would improve.

Then, in 1935, the Nuremberg Laws were passed: Jews were barred from voting and dismissed from civil service. They were prohibited from marrying Christians or having sex with them. Jews already married to non-Jews were to be tolerated, particularly if they were raising their children (known as *mischlinge*) as Christians. But henceforth, any Jew or Christian who defied these racial laws would be arrested, fined, and deported.

Frightened into obedience by the harshness of these new decrees, many Germans prevented their children from playing with Jewish classmates, fearing that any association at all with Jews could put them at risk. Jewish students in public schools were humiliated and shunned, as teachers taught "race science"—a pseudo-science claiming that Jews were an inferior race and had distinctive physical features. In Nazi textbooks and journals, Jews were portrayed as sinister-looking individuals with large, bulbous noses, dark, curly hair, menacing eyes, and funny-looking left ears. In contrast, true "Aryans"—Germans without any trace of Jewish blood—were portrayed as handsome, slim people with blond hair and blue eyes.

Of course, few Germans resembled either stereotype. Goebbels was short and dark-haired; Göring (Hitler's chief economic minister) had a large pot belly and was balding. Ellen Arndt, Lily Haber, and Evie Jacobson were blond. When Rosemarie Molser was a child, a teacher called her to the front of the class to show how the ideal "Aryan" looked!

In 1936 there was a brief hiatus in the persecution of Jews as the Nazis sought international attention by

Clockwise, from top left: Nazi students and SA unload "un-German" books for book burning, May 10, 1933. Burned-out synagogue of Aachen, Germany, after *Kristallnacht*. Jewish deportees march through a town in Lower Franconia on their way to a station to board trains for concentration camps.

hosting the Olympic Games. To welcome international visitors, they removed signs announcing that a town was free of Jews.

After the Olympics, life for the German Jews deteriorated further as Hitler began expanding his empire. In September 1938 he took the Sudetenland (the Czech Republic). The following March he annexed Austria, adding 6 million Austrians to his realm and imposing his harsh antisemitic restrictions on 200,000 Austrian Jews. In the following months, antisemitic restrictions increased: Many Jews were forced to give up their spacious homes and move into tiny, shabby apartments known as *Judenhäuser*. Jewish doctors were prohibited from treating non-Jewish patients; Jewish lawyers were disbarred. To identify themselves as Jews on their official documents, Jewish women had to add the middle name "Sara"; men had to add the middle name "Israel." Then, on October 28, the government expelled 17,000 Polish-born German Jews to a barren one-mile strip of land between Poland and Germany where there was almost no shelter or food.

Kristallnacht: **The Turning Point**

F OR MANY JEWS THIS EXPULSION WAS THE last straw. Upon hearing that his parents had been deported to this wasteland, Herschel Grynszpan, a young Jewish student living in Paris, shot a minor German official—Ernest vom Rath—believing him to be the ambassador. In protest, the Nazis organized a massive pogrom against all Jews in Germany and Austria.

On November 9 and 10, 1938, SA men and anti-semitic mobs swept through Austria and Germany, burning 1,000 synagogues, ransacking more than 7,000 Jewish-owned stores, and rounding up 30,000 Jewish men. The next morning the streets were filled with broken glass and rubble. On November 12, 1938, Jews were fined 1 billion marks for inciting the damage.

In the wake of this destruction, known as *Kristallnacht* ("the night of broken glass"), panic swept through Jewish communities as the Germans imposed harsher laws: Jews had to sell their businesses to non-Jews for a fraction of their value. Jewish children in German-run schools had to transfer to Jewish schools. Jews could not attend plays, movies, concerts, or art exhibitions. Jews were forbidden to drive cars, walk in certain areas, or attend universities. They had to turn in their securities and jewelry.

Leaving Germany and Austria became uppermost on every Jew's agenda. Many Jews enrolled in workshops to learn basic skills in fields likes dressmaking, carpentry, and toolmaking. Kurt Weinbach's father taught a class in watchmaking to Jewish men in Vienna. Even the most optimistic Jews, who had all along believed that the Nazi terror would pass, knew Germany was no longer safe: Almost 80,000 emigrated within the year following *Kristallnacht.* But many more Jews were trapped, unable to find hospitable countries. By the spring of 1939, France and Holland had closed their borders. Sweden, Denmark, and Switzerland were sending back Jews who arrived without proper papers. Even Palestine was off-limits after the British issued a White Paper on May 17, 1939, restricting Jewish immigration.

The U.S. continued to accept new émigrés, but

would not adjust its strict quota system to accommodate more Jews. It did not even fill its existing quota; officials frequently rejected applicants for technical reasons. Public opinion did not help: America was still recovering from its Great Depression and many citizens feared that more refugees would glut the job market and swell the welfare rolls. Antisemitism was another factor: A bias in favor of white American Protestant males made it difficult for many Jewish men to enter medical schools or join large U.S. corporations. While some American Jews agitated for more aggressive public actions, others were hesitant to get more involved in this "European" problem.

After the violence of *Kristallnacht,* a coalition of concerned citizens in England, Sweden, and Palestine arranged for orphanages and private citizens to take in children of German Jews and provide for them until their parents could join them or until the war ended. Bill Braun and Evie Jacobson both went to England on such *Kindertransports* (children's transports),

Clockwise, from top left: Jews at forced labor stand with shovels in a water-filled trench in Poland, 1940. Child working at a machine in a Kovno ghetto workshop, 1942. About 10,000 children under 19 were in the ghetto; almost half were killed. Below: Crematoriums at Auschwitz where Jewish corpses were burned after the victims were gassed.

DECEMBER 7, 1941	Japanese attack Pearl Harbor; U.S. officially enters World War.
DECEMBER 8, 1941	Jews deported to Chelmno, first extermination camp.
JANUARY 20, 1942	"Final Solution" to exterminate world Jewry drawn up by top Nazis in Wannsee, a Berlin suburb.
NOVEMBER 2, 1942	British defeat Rommel's troops at El Alamein in North Africa.
NOVEMBER 24, 1942	U.S. press learns of Final Solution; on Dec. 17, Allies condemn Nazis' "bestial policy" but do nothing.
FEBRUARY 2, 1943	German troops surrender at Stalingrad; decisive Allied victory. ▼

not knowing when—or if—they would see their parents again.

As competition increased for a dwindling supply of available visas, bribery became routine. Some Jews gave away their life savings to scam artists who promised them visas and delivered nothing. Even purchasing ship tickets was no guarantee, since many ships (like airplanes today) overbooked. Even after Warren Heilbronner's family received affidavits allowing them to enter the U.S., a German official made them sign over an insurance policy, worth 10,000 marks, to get final exit papers.

Jews became desperate, seeking refuge in any country that would accept them. China, Cyprus, India, Africa were often choices. The Habers fled Vienna hoping to settle in Palestine, but were marooned in Cyprus and then sent to Africa. Hermann Goldfarb traveled to Shanghai—alone—when he was only 19, not knowing if he would ever see his mother again. Kurt Weinbach and his parents traveled across the Soviet Union to China. The Taylor family traveled to Poland, Iraq, Turkey, and finally stayed in India. Rosemarie Molser conned her way to England as a domestic; then, fearing that Hitler would invade England, she emigrated to the Belgian Congo to join a man she knew only as a pen pal.

But they found difficulty even in some of these countries. After war broke out, Jews who had emigrated to England and other Allied countries were branded as "enemy" aliens, because they still had German passports. Bill Braun was sent to Canada from England and interned there. The Molsers were imprisoned and mistreated in a barracks in the Belgian Congo.

The Will to Survive

B Y FALL 1941, ALMOST THREE-FIFTHS OF Jews in the Reich had managed to emigrate, but there were still about 165,000 Jews trapped in Germany, and 60,000 stranded in Austria. New regulations prohibited Jews from owning radios, buying meat or even shaving cream. Then Hitler imposed a new humiliation: All Jews had to wear a yellow Star of David on the left side of their outerwear. In October, Jewish emigration was banned. From then on, Jews would either work as slave laborers in German munitions factories or they would be deported to "work camps" in the east, where millions of Jews from Poland, Russia, and the other occupied territories were being killed.

Erich and Ellen Arndt were among those Jews who were trapped in Berlin when they were only teenagers. They managed to stay alive by working twelve-hour days in factories for minimal wages. When America entered the war on December 7, 1941, the Arndts and many other Jews expected their luck to change soon: Hitler, they reasoned, could not possibly fight off the English, the Russians, and the Americans and would be overcome. Instead, Hitler intensified his war against the Allies—and the Jews.

In January 1942 Hitler and a team of top Nazis met at Wannsee, a Berlin suburb, and adopted the "Final Solution"—a plan to eliminate world Jewry. Deportations to the death camps began in earnest. Many Jews committed suicide as soon as they received deportation notices and the suicide rate in Germany and Austria skyrocketed.

By the following fall the war seemed to be turning in favor of the Allies. On November 2, 1942, the British defeated Field Marshal Erwin Rommel in a decisive battle at El Alamein in North Africa, igniting hopes that the war would soon end. By early December the embattled troops of Field Marshal Friedrich von Paulus were suffering heavy losses in the Battle of Stalingrad, the city that was the gateway to the Soviet Union. Everyone, including some of Hitler's closest advisers, thought the Reich was doomed. But Hitler refused to yield, ordering his troops to fight until they died, and ordering more Jews to the camps.

In Berlin, word spread that a major factory raid was planned; all Jewish slave laborers would be sent to concentration camps. Erich Arndt, only 19 at the time, feared that his loved ones would be caught up in the oncoming raid. He persuaded his father to go into hiding and seek help from his former non-Jewish patients. In January 1943, Erich, his sister, Ruth and their two parents went into hiding. In February, Erich's girlfriend, Ellen Lewinsky, and her mother, Charlotte, joined them. Then Bruno Gumpel, Erich's friend,

Top, left to right: A small group of partisans in the forests of Lublin, Poland. Partisans helped smuggle Jews across borders or hid them in the forest. Arrival of the *Marine Flasher* in New York Harbor, May 20, 1946. The ship was the first to carry Jewish refugees to the U.S. There were some 800 aboard.

APRIL 19, 1943	Warsaw ghetto uprising; thousands of Jews killed by Nazis.
JULY 25, 1943	Fall of Mussolini in Italy.
MAY 15, 1944	Over 400,000 Hungarian Jews sent to Auschwitz; most gassed on arrival.
JUNE 6, 1944	D-Day: Allies land in Normandy.
DECEMBER 16, 1944	Germans launch Battle of Bulge counter-offensive in Ardennes.
JANUARY 17, 1945	66,000 prisoners leave Auschwitz on Death March; 15,000 die en route.
APRIL 30, 1945	Hitler and Eva Braun commit suicide in Hitler's bunker in Berlin.
MAY 7, 1945	Germany's unconditional surrender to Allies, ending war in Europe.
AUGUST 6, 1945	U.S. drops first nuclear bomb on Hiroshima.
AUGUST 14, 1945	Japan surrenders to Allies. World War II is over.
DEATH TOLL:	5.8 million Jews killed by the Nazis, two-thirds of European Jewry.

■

joined the group. Miraculously, all seven survived.

When Paulus finally surrendered to the Russians at Stalingrad on February 2, 1943, it seemed to everyone that the war would soon be over. Yet between February 1943 and the end of the war in 1945, at least a million more Jews were murdered. Hitler seemed as intent on annihilating Jews as in winning the war, sometimes using trains to transport Jews to death camps instead of transporting supplies and ammunition to his soldiers. He also made sure that prisoners would not be rescued. When the Russians advanced toward the death camps in early 1945, Germans hurriedly evacuated them, sending barely living prisoners westward toward Germany on death marches. Thousands of Jews—ill, underfed, poorly clothed—died on these death marches. On April 30, Hitler committed suicide. Admiral Karl Doenitz was appointed his successor. On May 7, 1945, he ordered General Jodl to sign a document of unconditional surrender to the Allies. The war in Europe was over.

Against all odds, the Arndt group was still alive in Berlin. The Habers and the Molsers survived in Africa. The Goldfarbs and the Weinbachs were living in China, the Taylors in India. Bill Braun was in Canada. Evie Jacobson was living with her adopted family in England. Gerry Glaser and his father and the Heilbronners were safely in the U.S. Eventually, all would make their way to Rochester, New York, where they would build new lives, raise families, and contribute their expertise and wisdom to their community.

Barbara Lovenheim

Suddenly, He Was Nobody

The Story of Gerry Glaser

BY RONNY FRISHMAN

"One day, my friend Hanno came to me quite embarrassed," Dr. Glaser recalls. "His father had forbidden him to play with me—even to speak to me—because I was Jewish. This has stayed with me ever since."

GERRY GLASER, A THOUGHTFUL, SOFT-spoken physician in his mid-seventies, will never forget the phone call his family received on November 9, 1938. The hushed voice on the other end of the line delivered a shocking message: The Nazis were planning a major action against the Jews that night, and Gerry's father, Arthur—a prominent Berlin physician who had been confident he could "outlast" Hitler—was on the list of those to be arrested.

"My parents decided that Father would be safest if he spent the day in a movie theater," recalls Gerry, who was 13 at the time. "And since I was tall for my age, they were afraid I would become a target also; so my parents thought that I should accompany Father." Thea Glaser, Gerry's mother, would stay at home: "My

parents didn't think the Nazis would bother Mother."

Later that day, while Nazi mobs beat Jews and plundered their neighborhoods, uniformed men came searching for the doctor. Gerry and his father nervously sat out the fray in a darkened cinema. "I remember little of the movies—we must have seen several," says Gerry. "At one point, some men came in and shone some flashlights around, but we were not disturbed."

Gerry's uncle, Paul Benjamin, a manager at an international bank, was not so lucky; he was arrested and taken to a concentration camp. Later that evening, after calling home to see if it was safe to travel on the streets, Gerry and his father joined other relatives at his uncle's apartment, where they anxiously passed

Top: Gerry's mother, Thea, and his father, Dr. Arthur Glaser, with Gerry (age 8) and his sister, Gisela (age 13) in Berlin, 1933.

the rest of the night, pondering their options.

This was the night that would come to be known as *Kristallnacht*, "the night of broken glass." Daylight revealed the destruction: Broken glass filled the streets. The windows of Jewish shops had been smashed and covered with anti-Jewish signs. The large synagogue on Fasanenstrasse where Gerry had been bar mitzvahed only a few months before was in shambles.

"Father, by nature a stubborn man, finally decided that it was time to emigrate," Gerry says. "He decided that he wasn't going to outlast Hitler."

An Ordinary Family

BORN IN BERLIN IN 1925, GERRY, WHOSE given name was Gerhard, lived with his parents, Arthur and Thea, and an older sister, Gisela, in a spacious apartment on the Kurfurstendamm, a street in the fashionable center of West Berlin. Arthur Glaser had a large medical practice with two offices—one on the east side of the city, where he treated working-class people, and the other in his home, where he treated more well-to-do Berliners. Gerry's mother, Thea, was a "sweet, quiet lady" who had suffered from rheumatic heart disease for many years.

The family lived a comfortable, cultured life. They often visited their country's scenic areas, traveling freely around Germany, and they tended to spend their summer vacations in Italy, Czechoslovakia, or Yugoslavia. They had Jewish and non-Jewish friends; they felt very much a part of mainstream German society.

"Father was an energetic, successful, respected physician," Gerry recalls. "He considered himself very German, having served with distinction as a physician in World War I. He had been decorated for bravery and had been a prisoner of war in England. Because of this, the Nazis allowed him to practice medicine until quite late—1937 or 1938—after many

Get out!

A motorcyclist on the outskirts of a German village looks at a sign proclaiming "Jews are not welcomed here." Signs like these were placed in many cities and villages.

others had been deprived of their livelihood.

"My sister and I were largely raised by our maids, usually nice young girls from the country," Gerry says. "I have few memories of my elementary school years. Levels of instruction were high, education formal and rigid; we were expected to study Latin and French. Father was a well-trained violinist, and I was often taken to performances of the physicians' orchestra. There were also occasional chamber music evenings in our apartment."

Gerry undertook religious training and Hebrew lessons at the insistence of his maternal grandfather, Gustav Wolfsohn, a wealthy, devout man who had worked his way up from office boy to an executive position in a German manufacturing firm. "He was not a very nice person—he was demanding and domineering. We were all a bit afraid of him," Gerry acknowledges with a smile. When Gerry celebrated his bar mitzvah in Berlin's large liberal synagogue on

Fasanenstrasse, his grandfather—his only living grandparent—refused the seat of honor because the service was not Orthodox enough.

Set Apart

GERRY'S POLITICAL AWAKENING CAME when he was quite young—on his eighth birthday, January 30, 1933, the day Hitler came to power. "I was driving in the car with my father and I asked him about Hitler," recalls Gerry. "He said, 'It is a very bad thing.'" By 1935, the 'bad thing' had borne visible fruit; there were open displays of antisemitism by ordinary Germans. Gerry particularly remembers the Nazi posters on street corners that featured caricatures of Jews with long, hooked noses.

At his father's urging, Gerry joined a German Jewish youth group, *Bund der Deutsch-Judischen Jugend*, when he was about 11. The group gathered for sports,

Top, left to right: Gerry's father in WW I, 1916; Gerry's parents, 1918; Gerry's mother, Thea, with Gisela and baby Gerry, 1926; parents' wedding reception, 1918. Thea is fourth from left; Thea's brother, Berthold, is standing.

Gerry Glaser's political awakening came early—on his eighth birthday,
the day Adolf Hitler came to power. "I asked Father about Hitler," Gerry remembers.
"Father said, 'It is a very bad thing.'"

hikes, and singalongs. Once, during a hike into the countryside, some young men wearing the brown shirts of the Nazi SA ("storm troopers") stopped the group in the woods. The men questioned the group's leader, a youth about 16, and started to slap him around. The teen, who kept his hand over a pocket to hide a knife, didn't resist. "We were all in a panic—we just stood there," Gerry says. "After a while the men became bored and moved on, but the memory of total helplessness and fear remains strongly with me."

Gerry got a better understanding of what it meant to be Jewish when he entered the Fichte Gymnasium (a German high school). He was among three Jewish youths in his class. "I was fortunate," he says. "While not a great athlete, I did take part on our school relay running team and played on the handball team (a

German game similar to soccer) so I was largely left alone. One of the other boys, a quiet lad who looked like the Nazi caricatures of Jews, was not so fortunate; he underwent much hazing and some beatings.

"Some of the teachers became more strict and distant, while a few went out of their way to be nice to us. I particularly remember the music teacher ,who had the courage to say openly in class that it was a pity he could no longer teach the choir the beautiful melodies of Mendelssohn."

Gerry remembers a particularly hurtful incident involving a close friend, Hanno Ascher, who came from a wealthy Gentile family. The Aschers had a big, luxurious car and a private chauffeur, who would sometimes drive the youngsters around a nearby race-track. "One day, Hanno came to me quite embarrassed," he recalls. "His father had forbidden him to play with me—even to speak to me—because I was Jewish. This has stayed with me ever since."

Despite the growing anti-Jewish sentiment, some people provided acts of unexpected kindness. One afternoon, running to catch a bus home after a handball match in the suburbs, Gerry slammed into a car and was injured. Two SA men emerged from the vehicle and approached him; he was frightened. "But they were very nice to me, and they drove me home," Gerry says. They rang the Glasers' doorbell; Arthur Glaser opened the door and turned ashen. "There were the two Brownshirts and me with my face bleeding," Gerry says, now able to laugh at the memory. The officers left the badly bruised teen with his parents and calmly departed.

A Glimpse of the Future...
From Sachsenhausen

IN 1935, THE GLASERS HAD TO FIRE THEIR German servants because it was no longer legal for Jews to employ non-Jews. (It was considered *Rassenschande*, "racial shame," for a Gentile woman under the age of 45 to work for a Jew.) The Nazis eventually shut down Arthur Glaser's practice. "He had no income, and we moved to a smaller, simpler apartment," recalls Gerry.

No longer able to stay in the German secondary school, Gerry transferred to a Jewish school, where everyone was studying English. His sister, who was four years older, left Germany to study nursing in England. Gerry's uncle, Paul Benjamin, who had been transferred by his employer to Austria after Hitler rose to power, returned to Berlin in 1938. He had found the Austrian Nazis to be as antisemitic as the German Nazis. At one point, Paul's wife, Muschi, had been forced to scrub public streets in Vienna on her hands and knees.

The warning that saved Arthur Glaser from arrest on *Kristallnacht* was given at great personal risk by a young SA member who was the son of Frau Dust, a close friend of the Glaser family. She played the viola in the doctor's chamber-music group. But Uncle Paul did not get away: He was arrested and sent to Sachsenhausen, a concentration camp outside Berlin. There, many detainees were abused and tortured. Paul managed to escape this treatment by appearing to be working all the time.

Since the death camps were not yet set up, these early arrests and confinements were done primarily to pressure Jews to leave Germany. After Paul had been in Sachsenhausen for two weeks, his bank associates negotiated his release, promising authorities that the family would leave Germany. "My uncle came back dirty and smelly, and told us the way to survive was to look busy all the time," Gerry recalls. Soon afterward, the Benjamins emigrated to Holland. From there they went to England and then the U.S.

The American quota system made immigration difficult, but Arthur Glaser located some distant rela-

Opposite page: Gerry Glaser, in his home in Rochester at the age of 72.

tives—prominent New York lawyers—who agreed to sponsor his family. Since the Germans had imposed a heavy export tax on Jews as a way of getting their fortunes before they left the country, Jews had to smuggle money out. This was necessary not only to preserve their money but because English authorities would admit Jewish families only after being assured that they had the means to support themselves and would eventually be leaving to live in the U.S.

Gerry remembers the days before their departure: "The Nazis were very happy to let us leave. I believe they took some valuables and artwork, and there was a heavy penalty tax to be paid for leaving the country. The rest of our belongings were stored in large vans for future transportation. We never saw them again.

"When everything was in readiness, tickets bought, a few small suitcases packed, Mother became ill again and had to take to her bed. My parents jointly decided that she would stay behind under the care of her brother, Berthold Wolfsohn, a physician at the Berlin Jewish Hospital. She was to follow us to England as soon as she became well enough to travel."

But the family was never reunited.

Safety in the States

GERRY AND ARTHUR LEFT FOR ENGLAND on August 15, 1939. Since Germany was on the verge of declaring war on Poland, the British were suspicious of anyone who was German. They began rounding up some German Jewish refugees, thinking they might be German spies; Arthur Glaser was among those rounded up. He was interned at a camp on the Isle of Man. "Oddly enough, it wasn't a bad experience," notes Gerry. "He

seemed to have had quite a good time there. The men were well treated, and he became friendly with many artists and musicians."

Gerry, just 14, went to live with the Benjamins; then he moved around from house to house, living first with an English family and finally with an aged great-aunt from Austria who had an apartment near Hyde Park. He attended an English secondary school, where he learned to recite, in succession, all the British kings and queens.

On September 1, 1939, England declared war on Germany. The following August, 1940, the Germans sent massive numbers of bombers to pummel England. Gerry remembers the beginning of the London blitz (the bombing of London). Many Britons were killed or wounded during those bombing raids, but Gerry remained unscathed: "We would listen for the sound of planes and bombs, but I can't recall feeling very frightened," he recalls. "And nothing did happen to us."

That same month, Gerry and his father sailed for the United States, with less than $10 between them. They knew they would be met by Gerry's sister, Gisela, and the Benjamins, who had gone before them. For a while they lived with the Benjamins.

Though he was no longer wealthy, Paul Benjamin had secured a position at a New York bank. "My aunt saw to it that I was properly fed and clothed, and mothered me as I was growing up," Gerry says. Years later, when Arthur and Gerry were living on their own, Aunt Muschi would travel an hour by subway just to bring them home-cooked meals.

Gerry went to high school and worked at odd jobs. His father, who was in his fifties and not very fluent in English, had a more difficult adjustment; he had been a respected physician, but now he had to take mundane jobs as an ambulance attendant or a dishwasher. Eventually, however, Arthur passed the American medical boards and opened a small practice.

After graduating from high school in 1942, Gerry briefly attended Queens College; then he accepted a partial scholarship to Huron College, a small, Presbyterian school in Huron, South Dakota. "I have happy memories of Huron," he recalls. "One other young man, a Japanese-American, and I were the local curiosities, and we were both asked several times to speak to local groups of our experiences. My father later commented that I had become less shy and introverted after my year out there."

Return to Germany...
In the Conquering Army

IN 1943, GERRY WAS DRAFTED INTO THE U.S. Army as a medic. After the war, because he spoke German, he was stationed in Germany with the Counterintelligence Corps. This gave him a chance to look for his mother. His parents had exchanged letters once or twice a year through the Red Cross, but once the U.S. was at war with Germany, the letters had stopped, and neither Arthur nor Gerry had any idea where Thea Glaser was. Gerry's inquiries confirmed what Gerry had suspected, but dreaded to discover. In 1943, Thea had been sent to Theresienstadt,

a concentration camp in Czechoslovakia; from there she had been sent to Auschwitz. Gerry could get no definitive information about her, but he believes she died there, with her sister and brother-in-law. Thea's brother, Berthold Wolfsohn, continued to practice at the Berlin Jewish Hospital, which continued operating, under terrible conditions, all through the war. Somehow, he survived. He died in Berlin shortly after the war ended, but his wife and daughter made it to the United States. Gerry's grandfather lost everything to the Nazis and he died in Berlin during the war.

After Gerry left the military, he completed his studies at Columbia University. Then he enrolled in the University of Rochester Medical School, financing his studies with help from the G.I. Bill and part of an inheritance from his grandfather, obtained as reparations from the German government.

At a summer camp in Massachusetts in 1949, Gerry met Dorothy, a British-born artist who was to become his wife. They settled in Rochester and raised a family there; their son, John, is an associate professor of orthopedic medicine at the University of Iowa, and he has two children; the Glasers' daughter, Ann, lives in Rochester. Dorothy died in 1991.

Coming to terms with the past is still difficult for Gerry. He has visited Israel and Yad Vashem, the Holocaust memorial in Israel, but he will not return to Germany, and cannot bring himself to visit the Holocaust Museum in Washington, D.C. Despite his pain and loss, he believes that his experiences in Hitler's Germany influenced the way he chose to lead his life—inspiring him, in particular, to work for recognition for nurses and other caretakers of the sick and aged.

Even though he doesn't talk much about his past, thoughts about Auschwitz and the Holocaust increasingly weigh on his mind. "You never get rid of it," he says sadly. ✡

SS *St. Louis* stranded in Havana harbor with 900 Jewish German passengers aboard, May 27, 1939.

No Exit

Trapped in Nazi Lands

In the early years of Hitler's reign, it was relatively easy for Jews to leave Germany with their assets. Many who fled went to nearby countries—France, Belgium, and Holland—planning to soon return. In the mid-1930's Hitler increased antisemitic legislation, hoping to pressure more Jews to leave. But he forced them to leave their assets. He froze their bank accounts, prohibited them from transferring their money to foreign banks, and imposed steep exit taxes. Some Jews managed to smuggle valuables across the border. Even so, many were penniless when they reached their new homes.

After the *Anschluss* in March 1938, thousands of Austrian Jews joined the exodus. Recovering from the Great Depression, many countries feared that new refugees would burden their economies. In July 1938 they set up a world conference in Evian, France, with delegates from 32 countries to resolve the issue. Most deplored the rise of Nazism, but almost all—including the U.S.—refused to raise their Jewish quotas. After *Kristallnacht,* when many more Jews were desperate to leave, it became even more difficult to obtain visas. Attitudes in some countries actually hardened.

One tragic example occurred when on May 13, 1939, 900 German Jews surrendered almost all their assets to obtain passage and entry visas to Cuba. They sailed on the luxury liner, the SS *St. Louis.* When they arrived, the government refused to accept the refugees. Jews pleaded with the U.S. government to accept the stranded passengers, but to no avail. The *St. Louis* returned to Europe. En route, the American Jewish Joint Distribution Committee persuaded Great Britain, France, Belgium, and Holland to accept the refugees. A year later when Germany invaded France, Belgium and Holland, many passengers were trapped again. B.L.

Krist

November 9, 1938: Nazis burn synagogues, smash Jewish-o

Top, left to right: German children watch as a synagogue in Kuppenheiem, Baden Germany, burns during
Kristallnacht. Synagogue burns in Baden Baden.
Fragments of a synagogue in Lodz, Poland, destroyed
the next year. Bottom: Germans pass by the broken
shop windows of a Jewish-owned business
in Berlin that was smashed during *Kristallnacht.*

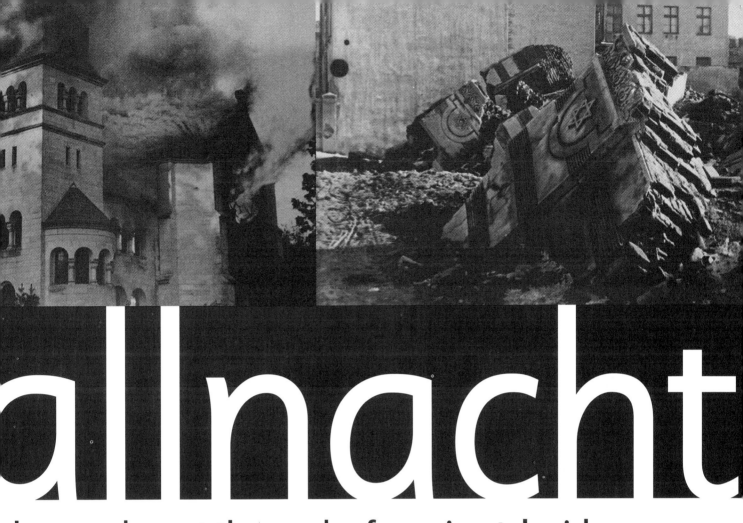

allnacht

shops, and arrest thousands of prominent Jewish men.

On October 28, 1938, the Nazis rounded up 17,000 German Jews who had been born in Poland and expelled them to a barren strip of land between Poland and Germany where there was little shelter. When Herschel Grynszpan, a 17-year-old Jewish student in Paris, discovered that his family had been sent to this no-man's-land, he went to the German Embassy on November 7 to shoot the German ambassador. By mistake, he killed a minor official. The Reich used the incident as an excuse to organize a massive pogrom against all Jews in Germany and Austria. On November 9 and 10, Nazi mobs, supported by storm troopers, set fire to 1,000 synagogues, vandalized and looted more than 7,000 Jewish shops and homes, and rounded up more than 30,000 Jewish men, many of them prominent. The next morning the streets were filled with shattered glass, giving rise to the name *Kristallnacht* ("the night of broken glass"). Jews were fined 1 billion marks to pay for the damage.

Profile No. 2

Escape to the Congo: A Memoir

BY ROSEMARIE MOLSER

When I was a student in Switzerland, I began corresponding with
a 30-year-old German Jewish doctor—Herbert Molser—who lived in
the Belgian Congo. At first I did not take Herbert's letters seriously.
After all, he lived far away and I was only 17. Then war broke out
and Herbert invited me to join him in Africa.

M Y FATHER WAS A BRILLIANT LAWYER IN
Bochum, Germany, who had served as an
officer in World War I. My mother was a
concert pianist. As a young girl I had blue eyes and
blond hair that I wore in braids. When Hitler came
to power and introduced "race science" into the curriculum, my teacher selected me to exemplify the
Aryan race! Soon after that I complained to my best
friend about how badly the Jews were treated by the
Nazis. She denounced me to the authorities and I was
kicked out of school. Realizing that my defiant nature
might put me at risk again, my parents sent me out
of the country to a convent school in Menzingen,
Switzerland. Later I transferred to a school in Geneva.

In the late 1930's my father could no longer

afford to send money to Switzerland for tuition, so I
decided to return home. But when the authorities re-
newed my passport, they stamped a "J" on it, identi-
fying me as a Jew. At the border I could be stopped or
sent to a concentration camp.

At a loss, I went to the nuns, who came to my
rescue: They tied my long hair on top of my head,
dressed me in a nun's habit, gave me a rosary, and sent
me away with their blessings. When I crossed the German border, no one even asked for my passport. No
one even recognized me when I walked into my parents' house! That was on November 2, 1938, just a
week before *Kristallnacht*. A month later, I was called
to Gestapo headquarters and informed that since I
had returned to Germany illegally, I had to leave

Top: Rosemarie's identity card, 1936. She was 16 years old.

I can never look at a gray November sky without remembering. I cannot listen to footsteps on wet pavement without remembering. On November 9, 1938, I lost my faith and my innocence. The land of my fathers rejected me forever. The culture that had nourished my family for centuries abandoned me.

I was only 17 years old on that rainy November night, but I still remember walking home from the hospital with my mother. The streets in Bochum, Germany, were deserted except for squadrons of marching Brownshirts. But something was different: Fear and apprehension hung in the air like an enormous storm cloud. When we got home, we listened to a report on the radio that a young Jewish boy had shot a secretary in the German embassy in Paris.

We had become accustomed to fear, but we now experienced overwhelming dread that the Nazis would retaliate. We went to bed and fell into an uneasy sleep until a phone call from a friend woke us: "They are ransacking all the Jewish stores," she blurted out. I immediately woke my mother.

Minutes later we saw fires all over the city. Then my sister and her family joined our vigil. We heard people screaming. Brownshirts had set fire to the synagogue. We were frightened that our home would be raided and my brother-in-law arrested. My sister and I took him to the train station on the other side of town, where he hid under the seats in the waiting room. By some miracle, my sister and I made it back to our parents' house. It was 6 a.m.

Suddenly, we heard glass breaking and wood splintering. Then a mob of some thirty men entered our house with hammers and axes. One sat at my mother's beloved grand piano and played the Horst Wessel song, the official song of the Nazi party; five others in riding boots trampled the sounding board into dust. In two hours of total madness, my parents' beloved art treasures, their many treasures—the memories of my happy childhood—all were destroyed.

The next morning, open lorries pulled up in front of every Jewish home. Brownshirts herded out all the men, young and old, who had not fled. Shouts, insults, and whips were freely applied to all who did not move fast enough. From my bedroom window, I waved good-by to my 17-year-old boyfriend. He was standing in an open truck. There was fear in his eyes as they took him away.

Rosemarie Molser

Kristallnacht

*When "race science" was introduced into the classroom, I was selected
to exemplify the Aryan race! But after Hitler came to power, my friend denounced me
for criticizing the Nazis, and I was kicked out of school.*

within six weeks—or go to a concentration camp.

I wanted to emigrate to England, but I was 18 and too old to be eligible for a *Kindertransport* (children's transport). There was only one possibility: to enter as a domestic servant. But agencies requested maids with experience. So my relatives fabricated an amazing list of household jobs and wrote letters of recommendation that I was a great maid. By the time they were through, I had aged ten years in two weeks. On paper I could cook and iron and clean like a demon. I landed a job in Buckinghamshire in the town of High Wycombe with the glorious pay of four pounds a month.

On February 9, 1939, I left Germany, scared to death of the future. I had learned Latin, Greek, and French in school, but I did not know any English. I was going to be a housekeeper, but I had never made a bed, held a broom, or set a table. I didn't know how to cook. I had almost no money. My parents took

me by train to Holland (a neutral country). There, we embraced for the last time. When the border patrol saw me crying, he gave me his hankie and said, "Be glad you are leaving, little girl. I wish it was me."

From Antwerp, we sailed to England. When we docked in Dover, I saw a stern, unsmiling woman carrying a sign with my name on it. I approached her and she started to walk away. So I grabbed my suitcases and ran behind her, trying to explain in German that I was Rosemarie Marienthal. We managed to board a train together to her home in High Wycombe. The ride was made in silence. It was a terrible beginning for both of us.

I thought everybody knew what Hitler was doing to the Jews. I expected love and understanding. But my employer—Mrs. Bathurst—was horrified to find a well-dressed, spoiled child instead of a robust German housekeeper. She and her husband had just returned from thirty years of government service in

Top, left to right: Rosemarie's father, Dr. Julius Marienthal, an officer in WWI, 1916; Rosemarie's house in Germany; Rosemarie (right) with her mother, Gertrude, her older sister Margarit (left), and her younger sister Heidi.

China. I do not believe they knew about the Nazis. Since I could not respond when she spoke to me in English, she thought I was deaf and started screaming at me. That made me even more uneasy and scared.

The Bathursts' cottage was another shock. I had grown up in a twenty-four-room mansion. Their cottage was tiny and had no heat; there were only two sinks of running water—no gas stove, no vacuum cleaner. The first night I was so cold that I slept in my coat and clothes. In the morning, the water in my sink was frozen, but I didn't know how to complain in English. I had to learn how to make a fire from sticks. Even worse, my employers expected me to cook all their meals.

Two days later I met a girl in the next cottage: She turned out to be an Austrian Jewish refugee who had also fled to England. Her English was good. She knew how to cook. We made an arrangement on the spot. I would clean all the floors and do all the dirty work in her cottage. In return, she would cook and iron for me in my cottage. We became good friends and helped each other.

Even so, life there was extremely hard. I was always hungry. My salary was meager. When I complained through my newfound friend, Mrs. Bathurst threatened to report me to the police and have me sent back to Germany. I didn't know if she would have, but she scared me. Into this atmosphere of total despair, weekly letters from Africa arrived. They kept me sane and hopeful.

My Dearest Herbert

WHEN I WAS A STUDENT IN SWITZER-land, I had begun corresponding with a 30-year-old German Jewish doctor named Herbert Molser. Herbert had treated my uncle in Germany; then he left for Zaire, Africa, in the Belgian Congo, to practice medicine. He wrote to my uncle that he was lonely there since he didn't know any single Jewish women. My uncle gave him my address and Herbert began writing to me. At first I did not take the letters seriously—he lived so far away and I was only 17 years old. There was a large age gap between us. But I answered his letters, and little by little, I began to like my new pen-pal. Herbert kept writing me in England, insisting that war was imminent and, since Hitler had already invaded Austria and Czechoslovakia, no country in Europe would be safe. He asked me to come to Africa. I could take care of his office and I would be safe from the Nazis. I knew he was right—Hitler might soon invade England—but how could I leave when my parents and younger sister were still living in Germany? It would cost a lot to get them out. My older sister had already emigrated to New York City, but her husband was ill and she had no money to spare.

I decided to learn English right away to get a better job. On my day off, I would go to the movies and sit through the same film all afternoon and evening. It was an unorthodox method for learning a language, but it eventually worked. I also read books and magazines—first with a dictionary and then without help. After six weeks, I could make myself understood. I went to the police station to find out if Mrs. Bathurst could really send me back to Germany. The police officer started to laugh. She couldn't. He told me to find another job and promised to help.

I managed to save six pounds and put an ad in *The London Times:* "French governess looking for a job with children." I landed a job with a lovely young family in Epsom in Sussex. Lily, the mother, had a 3-year-old girl and was pregnant. She treated me like family and became my friend. But her husband was an alcoholic, and when she wasn't home, I had to hide in my room because after a few drinks he was dangerous.

As the political situation in Germany deteriorated for the Jews, my family tried to leave, but they couldn't get visas to the U.S. and they didn't have enough money to enter England. Even though my mother had cousins in England, they were unwilling to help. They were ashamed of their German relatives.

Herbert became more insistent that I meet him in Africa. But I still hesitated. Leaving meant abandoning all hope of saving my parents and sister. Then, on September 1, 1939, war broke out between England and Germany and I could no longer communicate with my parents. In England I was considered an "enemy alien" because I had a German passport. I couldn't get an entry visa to America. Finally I decided to join Herbert in Africa. If I liked it, I would stay. If I didn't, I would try to get to America. I was too young and cocky to realize the possible dangers of going to Africa, and I wouldn't listen to anybody who didn't agree with me.

My next problem: I could get to Belgium, still a neutral country, by train, but I didn't have enough money for a plane ticket from there to Africa. Herbert surprised me and sent me a ticket! Then more problems: I could leave England, but I couldn't get a visa to return. I decided to take my chances and go anyway. Then the Belgian authorities wouldn't give me a visa—they didn't want any more German Jewish refugees in Belgium. I camped on the steps of their consulate for two days, pleading with them for a visa. When they finally realized I would not leave, they finally gave me a transit visa.

I felt as if I had won a major battle. My lovely English family took me to the ferry in Dover, and we exchanged emotional farewells. I never saw them again. During the blitz in 1940, they were all killed by German bombs. God held me in his hand again. If I had stayed in England, I would not be here today to tell my story.

To Africa, in Desperation

THE CHANNEL CROSSING IN 1939 WAS ANother nightmare. There were English mines in the channel, intended to hit German U-boats. Nobody, not even our ferryboat captain, knew exactly where the mines were. We might not get to Belgium alive. We had to wear Mae West lifesaving vests and keep our belongings on us. We couldn't go below. We ate as we stood on deck, shivering with cold and fear. But we were so scared we didn't even get seasick in the choppy waters. When we finally saw the bright lights of the port of Antwerp, we cheered and held hands and embraced each other

Waiting for me on the pier was my aunt. "Rosemarie, call your parents immediately," she said. In Brussels, I did just that. But it was a terribly angry confrontation. My parents did not want me to go to Africa to meet Herbert. He was too old; I was too young. They tried to dissuade me. Finally, when they realized I would not change my mind, they reluctantly gave me their blessing. When I think now about that last conversation with my father, I am ashamed to think how selfish I was and how little understanding I showed for his agony.

The next day I went to the airline office to confirm my flight to Africa. But I ran into new problems. The French would not allow me, a German national, to fly over their country without special permission. I told them I was not carrying bombs or even a camera—all to no avail. So I marched off to the French Consulate. "Out of the question," I was told. "You cannot sit in an airplane flying over France. You could be a German spy taking pictures of vital installations. Don't bother. Go away."

I left, feeling the world closing in on me again.

Opposite page, left to right: Herbert Molser as a child with his grandfather, 1911; Herbert (second from right) in medical school in Berlin, 1930. Rosemarie in the U.S., 1946.

*When we arrived at his house, Herbert went off on an errand
and I closed the door and cried. I didn't want to marry this man I had just met,
but I didn't want to be sent back to Germany. I had no choice.*

What next? I had heard that there were ships going to Africa. So off I went to the Belgian Ticket Agency. I asked for a ticket on the next ship.

Everybody laughed. "Mademoiselle, don't you know there is a war in Europe and everybody is trying to get out? We have no stateroom or other space for six months."

At that point I began sobbing so hard that I frightened everybody there. They tried to calm me, but I couldn't stop crying. All of a sudden a man behind me said, "Stop and listen."

I looked up and saw a young Catholic priest gazing at me with such understanding and kindness that I pulled myself together. The office became so silent that you could hear a pin drop.

"My child," he said, "you have your whole life ahead of you. I am going to the Congo to serve in my parish. You are trying to save your life. If I get caught by the Germans, I don't think anything will happen to me. But if the Nazis catch you, terrible things will

happen. I will give you my ticket to Africa. Take my place on the next boat, and God be with you."

Before I could respond, he shoved the ticket into my hand and disappeared into the crowd. God works in mysterious ways.

On September 25, 1939, I boarded a ship, the *Leopoldville*, for Africa. I shared a stateroom with two older Belgian girls. We soon discovered we were the only women aboard—among 300 Belgian men on their way to jobs in the Congo. After a few days we relaxed and had a wonderful time, dancing and partying. I managed to forget my misery and crammed my whole teenage years into those two short weeks.

When our ship docked in Matadi, Africa, I took a train to Leopoldville, then the capital of the Belgian Congo. Herbert had left a welcoming call in my hotel. Reality set in and I began feeling overwhelmed by the enormity of my adventure. The next day, I boarded a riverboat headed for Stanleyville to meet Herbert. When we arrived two weeks later, I saw

Herbert standing on the dock. My legs barely carried me off the boat. Both of us will always remember those first awkward moments. He wanted to kiss me hello and I turned my head away. Not an auspicious beginning.

Then I got into his car—a little Oldsmobile convertible. After we'd been driving for about five minutes, a woman stopped him: *"Mon enfant est malade; je veux vener set après-midi à votre office."* ("My child is sick. I want to come to your office this afternoon.")

"You cannot come. I'm getting married," he said.

"What?" I responded, shocked at the disclosure.

"Don't you know? Didn't you get my letters? I wrote to you at every port stop."

"What letters?" I replied "I didn't get them."

He explained that the Belgian government had new rules: Foreign women entering the Congo had to show that they were financially self-sufficient, or they had to get married within 48 hours. Since I had no official permission to return to England and no means to support myself, Herbert had decided to marry me, so I could stay there legally. And since this was Friday and offices were closed on Saturday and Sunday, we had to get married by 4 p.m. Otherwise, I would be sent back to Germany.

When we arrived at his house, Herbert went off on an errand and I closed the door and cried. I didn't want to marry a man I had just met, but I didn't want to go back to Germany either. I had no choice. During the wedding ceremony, Herbert nudged me to say *"Oui"* (yes) when it was time. Then we went home

and opened a bottle of champagne. Ten minutes later I fled into a room and closed the door for several days. I couldn't even call my parents, because I knew they would be so angry. When I finally emerged, I called Herbert's parents in Germany, knowing they would be happy for us. Herbert continued to be patient. One night there was a big thunderstorm and I got very scared. I went to him for comfort, and that's when we finally, really got married.

Toughing It Out in the Belgian Congo

THE CLIMATE WAS HUMID AND HOT MOST of the time, and we had no fans or electricity. I spent my days in a bathtub to keep cool, but there was often no water. I still didn't know how to cook, and when I tried, the heat in the kitchen overwhelmed me. I didn't know anyone and our political position was still very difficult. Even though we were Jewish, we were officially German, and, therefore, disliked by the Belgians: Germany had the reputation of having done horrible things to the Belgians during World War I. There were no other Jewish families in the town; the only friend I could make was the German wife of a Belgian officer.

I also worried about my family in Germany. I knew from their letters that Jews were having a rough time. My father was still practicing law, but two other Jewish families had moved into our house. Everyone was trying to get out of Germany, and visas were hard to find.

Top: Rosemarie and Herbert Molser as newlyweds in Africa, on Rosemarie's 21st birthday.

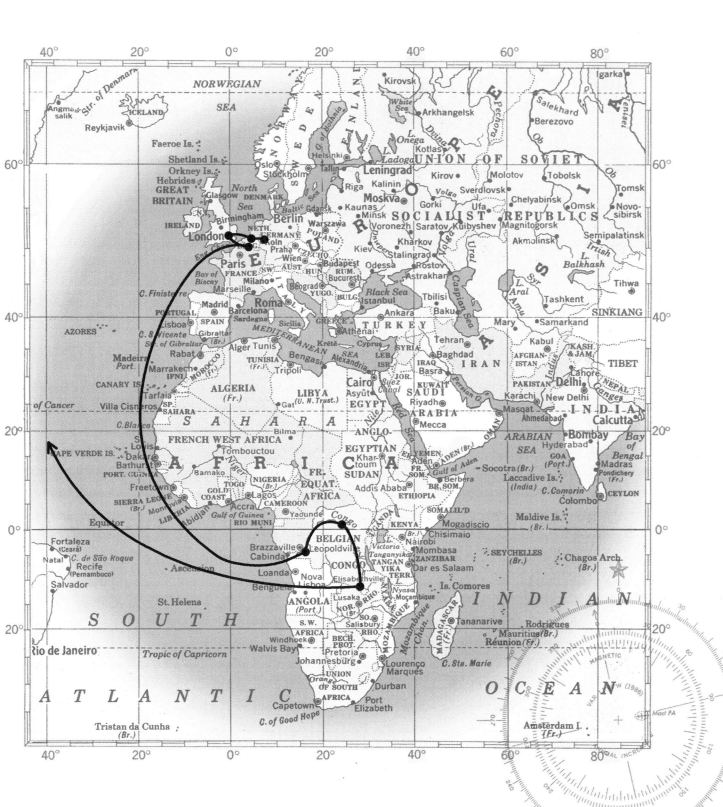

From Germany, Rosemarie took a train to Holland, and sailed to England in 1938. The next year she fled to Belgium, hoping to find passage to Africa to meet Herbert Molser, the man she was destined to marry. From Brussels she sailed to Matadi, took a train to Leopoldville, then a riverboat on the Congo to Stanleyville in the Belgian Congo. In 1941 she and Herbert moved south to Elizabethville and lived there until the war ended. From there, they flew to the U.S.

Life soon changed for us as well. Germany invaded Belgium and Holland on May 10, 1940. The next morning, the man who had married us showed up and took Herbert. When I found out that Herbert was in jail. I stormed over and said, "What is going on? We are Jews. We have 'J's on our passports!"

"That doesn't mean anything to me," answered the officer. "Your passport is German, and you are *enemy aliens* now."

I went back home feeling desolate. I had no money to buy food. I couldn't even get payment from Herbert's patients. I spent the next six weeks worrying and virtually starving. Finally, I went to visit Herbert, and the administrator told me he was gone. I was so weak from hunger and so scared that for the first time in my life I fainted. When I woke up, they told me that Herbert was in a camp and I could join him. Since I had no money and no food, I didn't see another choice. But I couldn't even pack a suitcase. Instead, I had to put my precious belongings in a sheet.

In the camp, Herbert and I lived in a hut with a corrugated roof. The heat was unbearable. They locked us in at 6 p.m. and let us out at 8 a.m. Since we had only a narrow cot, one of us slept on the floor. We had no food. We made a horrible soup from leaves off the trees, oil, and manioc, a root used by the Africans to make flour and cooked over four sticks of wood on the ground. We were surrounded by other German prisoners of war who disliked us because we were Jewish. We were scared to death.

When Italy entered the war in June, the Belgians opened another camp for Italian POW's, and they asked Herbert to be the medical supervisor of both camps. Two months later, I got appendicitis and was taken to a hospital. The surgeon there performed an appendectomy, but he was such a butcher that I developed a severe infection and it ruined my childbearing abilities. I spent the next two months recovering in a hospital ward, and they wouldn't even let Herbert visit me.

When I returned to our camp, I weighed only 90 pounds. During a Red Cross inspection, a nurse demanded that Herbert and I be moved. "It is against all international regulations to keep you here," she said. Since the southern part of the Congo was farther away from the equator and not nearly as hot, they moved us to a town near Elizabethville. The trip took three weeks, and when we arrived I was still sick and

Top, left: The Molsers' marriage book, October 25, 1939. Top, right: The riverboat *Reine Astord* that sailed from Leopoldville to Stanleyville, Belgian Congo. Opposite page: Rosemarie and Herbert Molser in Rochester.

had to be hospitalized. Four weeks later, they moved us to a small town, Biano, where we were classified again as "enemy aliens."

There we had to share a house with a Swiss/Austrian couple who were vicious antisemites. They called us names and schemed to steal our food, which was only a large pot of soup made from meat, some potatoes, and some vegetables. One day they called me away from the house and fed the entire pot of soup to their dogs. It was our meal for the entire week! When I saw the empty pot I cried. Luckily, a Red Cross officer was inspecting the camp.

"What is wrong?" he said.

When I told him what had happened and that Herbert was a doctor, he called the head surgeon of a large company in Elizabethville and told them to hire Herbert. They did. We arrived in May 1941 and spent the rest of the war living there. Herbert was the head of a 120-bed hospital, and we had a pleasant house. The worst was over for us—but not for our families.

By that time, my parents had managed to emigrate to America, but Herbert's parents were still in Berlin, living in a crowded *Judenhaus* [a house for Jews only]. They had little money, and we could communicate with them only through the Red Cross. There was nothing we could do for them. In 1942 we got what turned out to be their last message. Then there was silence.

When the war ended, in May 1945, we had to make a decision. Berlin was now in ruins and we couldn't get any news of Herbert's family. Finally, we decided to emigrate to America. After more mishaps, we got on a DC-4 propeller plane that took three days to fly to New York City.

Reunion in the U.S.

IN NEW YORK WE REJOINED MY MOTHER AND two sisters. My father, sadly, had died the previous year. Then we found out why we had stopped hearing from Herbert's parents: Upon receiving a deportation notice to go to a concentration camp, they had hanged themselves. We were all devastated by the news, even though on some level we knew they had done the best thing for themselves.

Herbert threw himself into studying for his American boards. I took a job as a nanny, working eighty hours a week. We rented a room in Washington Heights, in northern Manhattan, where many other German Jews had settled. We enjoyed the culture and excitement of New York City. A year later, we decided to settle in Rochester, New York, because it had a top medical school, a Philharmonic orchestra, and it was a good place for families. Since I couldn't bear children, we adopted a boy, Bruce, and a daughter, Kathleen. Kathy married and had two children; then, in 1994, she died from illness. My beloved Herbert died recently at the age of 92. We had been married almost 61 years. My husband helped me grow up; I helped him as he grew old.

My life has been a mix of tragedy and happiness. I miss my daughter and my parents. Life is not the same without my beloved husband. But I enjoy my son and grandchildren. I have come to realize that we can survive fear and cruelty and still remain loving and forgiving. To judge is easy; to remain human is difficult. I almost perished because of the cruelty of many, but I survived because of luck and the goodness of some. ✡

Profile No. 3

Without a Live Sponsor

The Story of Warren Heilbronner

BY MICHAEL WENTZEL

Even in 1939, when they were forcing Jews out of Germany, the Nazis put up formidable obstacles to escape. If families could not take any money with them, how could they survive in an alien land?

WERNER HEILBRONNER (WHO CHANGED his name to "Warren" in the U.S.) was born in Stuttgart, Germany, on November 7, 1932. His father, Helmut was a textile engineer; his mother, Dora Loeb Heilbronner, was the daughter of a well-to-do industrialist who owned Gebrüder Loeb (The Brothers Loeb), a large knitting mill that manufactured men's underwear. The company was founded by Dora's grandfather. Dora's father, Hermann Loeb, thereafter operated it with his brothers. When Dora married Helmut, he joined the firm as the factory superintendent.

The Heilbronners were well-off and lived in a large, mansion-style home which they rented in a well-to-do area of the city. "My mother played tennis and bridge and enjoyed the social scene," recalls Warren. "Until we came to America, she never cooked a meal, never washed any dishes, never cleaned any clothes. She had a Christian maid, Marie Schied, who eventually risked her life for my grandparents."

While there appeared to be little antisemitism in Stuttgart in the early 1930's, the Heilbronners—like many Jews in Germany—associated primarily with other Jews. They thought of themselves as separate, but not unequal. They did not feel insecure or in danger. Even after the passage of the Nuremberg Laws in 1935 and the tightening restrictions against Jews, the family did not think it would be dangerous to remain

Top: Brother Leslie, Mother Dora, and Warren in Stuttgart, circa 1937. Opposite page: Warren, one-and-a-half years old.

in Germany. "I was only a small child and I didn't feel the restrictions," recalls Warren. "I had no sense of the world coming apart, since my parents sheltered me and my brother, Ludwig. In my little world, the restrictions only meant that I didn't go to kindergarten, and that my friends and I played in each other's houses. What happened in the world of politics was kept far away from us."

"Like many Jews, we had a comfortable life," he continues. "We were Germans first. This was our country, our homeland. 'We've gone through tough times,' everybody thought, 'but this will pass.' We didn't feel the kind of pressure that Jews felt in other cities where there was more outward antisemitism. However, in the fall of 1936, as a precaution, on the advice of a friend, my father went to the U.S. Consulate in Stuttgart and applied for a number for entry into the United States."

On July 19, 1938, the family received a document from the consulate in Stuttgart stating that they were number 5,442 on the waiting list. They were told to get the necessary papers together. By the beginning of November 1938 all requirements for entry into the United States had been met, with the exception of the affidavit of support that Helmut's uncle Max, a successful Realtor from Memphis, Tennessee, had agreed to provide. Such an affidavit could come only from a sponsor—an American citizen who promised to be financially responsible for the proposed immigrants.

Then on November 9, 1938, Nazi Brownshirts swept through all German cities, smashing Jewish businesses, burning synagogues, and arresting as many Jewish men as

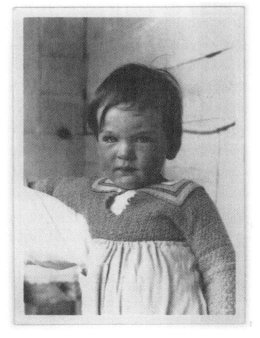

they could find. It was *Kristallnacht*.

During the night, they arrested Dora's father and took him into custody. When Helmut found out, he realized the Gestapo might come looking for him as well; he decided to hide with Dora's mother, believing that the Gestapo would not return there.

"About 5:30 the next morning, the knock came on our door," recalls Warren. "They were looking for my father. My mother said, 'He is not here.' So they searched our house. As soon as they left, my mother sent my brother to warn my father that the Gestapo was looking for him."

Not wanting to leave the factory unprotected, Helmut had gone there to make sure it was safe. The Gestapo found him there and arrested him. Both Helmut and Dora's father Hermann were soon transferred from Stuttgart to Dachau, an internment camp for political prisoners, that subsequently became a brutal Nazi concentration camp.

The Key Word: "Max"

SHORTLY AFTER ARRIVING IN DACHAU, Helmut sent his wife a brief postcard: "Dear Dora," he began. "I am here since Friday and I am all right. Don't worry about me. Every week you can send me 15 marks. But mention the exact address on the other side. Greetings to you. Lutz, Werner, Parents, Mother, and Max. Yours, Helmut."

"Max" was the key word. Dora knew that mentioning Max's name in the postcard was a signal for her to write to him immediately to obtain the affidavit of support, the missing piece that would enable

In early December Dora received the affidavit and she took it directly to the police, who agreed to release Helmut. By this time he had been in Dachau for almost five weeks. There he witnessed how brutally the Nazis treated all the prisoners. Inmates were harassed, underfed, and mistreated; many elderly men died there. One night Helmut managed to sneak through the guards into the barracks where his father-in-law was held to make sure he was all right, even though Helmut risked being shot for going outside of his section. On another occasion a prisoner was taken sick. Helmut and a fellow prisoner volunteered to take him to the infirmary. When they arrived there, the man in charge of the infirmary asked, "What do you want?" They said, "The man needs treatment." Then Helmut and his friend were ordered to leave. As they turned to go, they looked around and saw a whole stack of bodies piled up like cordwood in the back of the infirmary.

the Heilbronners to leave. But unbeknownst to Helmut, the affidavit had arrived at the post office soon after he had been arrested, sent there by registered mail. Dora went to the post office to pick it up.

"Sorry, it is addressed to Helmut," the clerk responded. "You can't have it. Registered mail can only be picked up by the addressee."

"In 1938, Dachau was a harassment camp: Jews were interned there to scare them into leaving Germany. Hitler wanted to take all their money and make them a burden on the rest of the world."

Dora persisted for three days. "Every hour or half-hour she would go to the window to ask for it," Warren recalls. "And they would say no. So my mother wired Sigmund, another uncle, and asked him to have Uncle Max send another affidavit—this time addressed to her." When Sigmund received the wire, he wrote directly to the Assistant Postmaster General in Washington, D.C., requesting that the U.S. post office intercede with the German authorities to release the letter to Dora, because, as he said, 'the papers contained in this registered letter might enable her to get a release of her husband, Helmut Heilbronner, from Concentration Camp.' This letter was to no avail. Eventually a second affidavit was sent directly to my mother."

A New Nightmare

ONCE HELMUT WAS RELEASED, THE FAMILY prepared to emigrate. "Then in January my grandmother [Helmut's mother] died from illness," recalls Warren. "We had applied for our visas to enter the U.S., but still had to wait for our number to come up. Right up to the very end we didn't know whether we were going to make it or not. For my father, it was a nightmare.

"Finally, in late January 1939, we were advised that we would be admitted into the U.S. But when my father went to the German embassy to pick up papers that would allow our family to leave Germany, more difficulties followed. The officer blackmailed him. 'It will cost you 10,000 marks,' he said. My father had already been forced to give over all his money to the Reich and he didn't have more," recalls Warren. "The officer persisted. My father remembered that he still owned a life insurance policy which had a cash surrender value of 10,000 marks. But when he went to the insurance company to try to cash it in, he was told: 'You're a Jew. We can't cash this. We can't give you any money.'"

When Helmut relayed the news to the officer who was blackmailing him, the officer told him that he would call the insurance company and authorize it to issue my father a check. "Then bring it back," the officer demanded. "If you're not back in a half an hour, you can forget about your visa."

After meeting the officer's demand, Helmut received the German exit visa. The family could finally emigrate [to the United States]. This was the moment he had planned for ever since he had applied for the exit number. Realizing that he might not be able to take money out of the country, he had made several visits to his Aunt Frieda, who lived in Lausanne, Switzerland. Each time he went he smuggled jewelry with him that he hid in the hubcap of his car, so Frieda could keep it for him. He would thereby have some available resources if and when he got out.

Helmut and his brothers also devised another plan to send assets out of Germany. Helmut's mother, who had died in 1939, had left her three sons a small inheritance. The brothers knew the

government would take the money when they emigrated, since Jews were not allowed to leave Germany with any cash. They also knew that Germans always followed the law.

"So my father and his two brothers decided to renounce their inheritance," Warren explains. "In doing so, my grandmother's brother, Sigmund, who lived in the U.S., became the beneficiary, since he was the next living relative." The boys agreed that if they got the money out they would divide the money four ways; Helmut's uncle, Sigmund, would get a quarter for being the shill; Helmut and his two brothers would each get a quarter. "Our plan worked," he recalls. "The German government honored the renunciation and released the inheritance to my uncle."

Bluffing

JUST BEFORE THEY PLANNED TO GO TO THE U.S. Consulate to pick up their final papers, they faced another potential obstacle. Helmut learned that his uncle, Max Heilbronner, the family's sponsor, had died on January 10. It was now February 1939. Would the U.S. officials find out that the

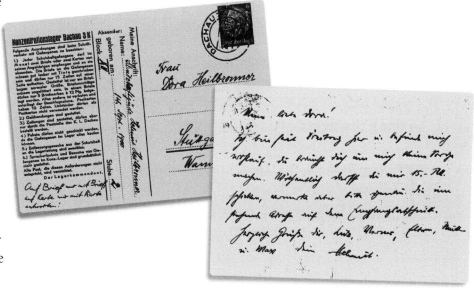

Opposite page: Dachau Concentration Camp. This page: Postcard that Helmut sent Dora from Dachau with code word "Max" on it.

*"What I went through had a powerful impact on me. What millions of Jews
endured during the Holocaust has a very significant place in history.
It shows that a government gone amok can threaten to destroy an entire people."*

Heilbronners' sponsor was no longer alive? With much trepidation, the family went to the consulate.

"When they asked us where we were going to go, I was supposed to answer, 'Memphis, Tennessee,'" recalls Warren. "But I said, 'Tennessee Memphis.' The officer said, 'I also come from Memphis, Tennessee.' My father's face went sheer white because Max Heilbronner was well-known in the community. He was worried that this official might have seen Max's obituary in the Memphis newspaper. But we were fortunate. He was not aware of Max's death."

Leaving Stuttgart

THE HEILBRONNERS FINALLY LEFT STUTTGART on March 3, 1939. Warren, only six-and-a-half, was excited at the prospect of traveling to a new country, but soon learned that it could be treacher-

ous. "We went by train and had our own compartment," he recalls. "There were lots of Jewish families there. When we got to the Swiss border, the Germans checked papers. They passed on ours. But they took the family behind us and we never learned what happened to them.

"We were at risk until we crossed the border," he continues. "Since my brother Ludwig had been sick the day before we left, my mother put rouge on him so they didn't think he was too ill to travel."

In Lausanne, Switzerland, Helmut retrieved his jewelry from his aunt. Then they visited Helmut's brother in Paris. From there they traveled to Rotterdam and boarded a ship for New York City.

When the Heilbronners arrived in the U.S., they had only a scant sum of money from Helmut's jewelry and inheritance. They settled in Perry, New York, because there was a major textile factory there, and

Top, left to right: Heilbronner residence at 2 Wannenstrasse, Stuttgart, Germany; Postcard depicting the Gebrüder Loeb factory in Stuttgart; Bombed out factory after World War II; Warren and Joyce Heilbronner in Rochester, November 2000.

Helmut got a job in textiles, earning $12 a week. Once in the U.S., Helmut changed his name to 'Harry', Ludwig's to 'Leslie' and Werner's to 'Warren.' "My father didn't want us to be raised with German names while the war was still going on," says Warren. "It was bad enough to be one of the few Jewish families living in a small town."

The Relatives Left Behind

IN JUNE OF 1939, THE NAZIS TOOK OVER THE family's factory by sending over one of their lackeys to take charge. "My grandfather had to send a letter to customers thanking them for their patronage and introducing them to the new owner," recalls Warren.

While the grandparents remained there, also waiting to leave, they were aided by Marie Schied, the maid who had worked for Dora. "She hated the Nazis," says Warren. "When our family left for America, Marie returned to her family who lived in a small village in the Black Forest. But she would sneak into Stuttgart and bring food to my grandparents, who otherwise would have had very little to eat. She took great risks to do this. If she had been caught, she would have been shot."

The Heilbronners brought Marie to the U.S. for a visit in 1960 as a way of showing their gratitude to her. "Marie was then in her eighties, and when she arrived at our home, she looked at our kitchen floor and got down on her knees and started scrubbing the floor until my mother stopped her. She still thought of herself as a maid. But now she was our guest," recalls Warren. "We would have arranged for her to stay, but if she became sick, there was no way to get medical insurance for her."

Warren eventually became a lawyer and settled in Rochester with his wife, Joyce. They have three sons. His son Larry, Vice President of Finance for Canandaigua National Bank, and Larry's wife, Laura, have two children, Madeleine and Sam. Son Jerry, a systems analyst with Raytheon, and his wife, Lisa, have three children, Sarah, Brian, and Heather. Son Kevin works for a public relations firm in Washington, D.C., where he is also the public address announcer for the NBA and NNBA teams.

Reflecting on his experience, Warren remarks, "My family's trauma was minimal compared with what other German Jews suffered. But it had a powerful impact on me. It shows that a government gone amok can threaten to destroy an entire people, and that we must always be vigilant." ✡

Right: Children of first *Kindertransport* arriving in Harwich, England, December 2, 1938.
Far right: Children on deck of SS *Batory* in Melbourne, Australia, 1940. Below: On deck of SS *Orama,* en route to Australia, 1939.

Kindertr

Over 10,000 Jewish children under 18 were sent for safeke

ansport
to homes in England, Palestine, Australia, and Sweden.

Kindertransports were "children's transports" organized by Jewish and non-Jewish organizations after *Kristallnacht* to provide sanctuary in unoccupied countries for Jewish children from Austria and Germany. Children had to be under the age of 18 and their parents had to send them, a decision that usually turned out to be wrenching for everyone. Parents knew they might never see their children again, and the children were not used to being separated from their families. But the grown-ups knew that living abroad was safer than staying under Hitler's rule. Between 8,000 and 10,000 children went to England; 3,400 went to Palestine under the auspices of *Youth Aliya* (a Zionist program that brought young people to Palestine). Thousands more went to Sweden, Denmark, Belgium, and Australia. One thousand came to the U.S.

In England and the Low Countries, youngsters were placed in children's homes or with foster families; in Palestine, most lived on kibbutzim (co-operative communities). Parents hoped to join their children when the war was over. But, tragically, many parents died in concentration camps. Some children who went to Belgium and Denmark were also captured when the Germans invaded those countries. A few lucky children were reunited with their parents after the war; some orphaned children were adopted by their foster families; many others had to fend for themselves as they grew up.

Who Am I?

Evie Jacobson:

Kindertransport Child

BY MARK LIU

"Mischlinge"—children of one Jewish parent and one non-Jewish parent—were not treated as severely by the Third Reich as children of two Jewish parents, particularly if they were brought up as Christians. So Evie's parents raised her as a Lutheran, even baptizing her in the Evangelical Lutheran Church.

EVELIESE SHUERMANN JACOBSON, A SLIM, gracious, fair-haired woman, was born in Hildesheim, Germany, in 1929. She still remembers the event that changed her life. She was only 9 years old when a classmate come up to her and yelled, "Your father's a dirty Jew! Your father's a dirty Jew!"

"He is not!" challenged Evie, a beautiful blond-haired, blue-eyed child who had been raised as a Christian and baptized in the Evangelical Lutheran Church.

When Evie ran home to tell her mother, Else, what had happened, her mother realized that she couldn't easily keep the truth from her daughter any longer. Else told Evie that she (Else) had been born a Catholic; but Evie's father—Otto—was Jewish.

The news meant only one thing to the young child: She was one of Germany's unwanted.

"It's not true, it can't be true," Evie cried. "I hate you, I hate my father!"

It was 1938 and antisemitism was at a peak. Evie was a student in a typical German school where her classmates saluted "Heil Hitler" every day and sang the German national anthem. Her teachers, required by Nazi law to teach "race science," taught Evie and

Top: Evie at the age of 9 in Hildesheim, Germany, spring 1939.

Opposite page: Evie in England with Philip and Lois Whyatt, the children of her foster family, September 1939.

40   Perilous Journeys *Jacobson*

her classmates that Jews were an inferior race and that they were enemies of the Third Reich.

In an attempt to protect their daughter from the inevitable slurs and self-doubts that would arise from hearing these vile lies about the Jewish people, the Shuermanns had decided to withhold her father's Jewish identity from Evie. They wanted to bring her up in the most normal environment possible. They visited frequently with Else's brother, Fritz, and his wife, who were Christian. Finally, as antisemitism became more and more virulent, they decided to make Evie's Christianity official: In 1938 they baptized Evie in the Evangelical Lutheran Church. Evie was 9 years old.

There was also a practical reason for their deception: *"Mischlinge"*—children of one Jewish parent and one non-Jewish parent—were not treated as severely by the Third Reich as children of two Jewish parents, particularly if they were brought up as Christians. Evie might not ever be subject to the same terrible restrictions that were being levied upon children with two Jewish parents.

Evie's parents explained all this in a patient, caring way. Eventually, her anger dissipated. But she could not foresee that—as a result of this revelation—her life was about to change dramatically. Even though she would not suffer the brutalities of the concentration camps, she would throughout her life

go through painful conflicts about who she was and who her true parents were.

Flight to England

AS THE NAZIS IMPOSED MORE AND MORE restrictive measures on Jews, Evie's parents made plans to emigrate to England; Else got a job as a housekeeper, Otto as a butler. Then, tragically, in March of 1939, Else died of tuberculosis. Shortly afterward, Evie's Uncle Fritz, a Nazi party member, cut off relationships with Evie, no longer wanting any association at all with relatives who were partly Jewish. Otto, realizing that he had to get Evie out of Germany as soon as possible, arranged for her to leave on a *Kindertransport* (a children's transport) to England. He planned to join her as soon as he found a job there.

The following August, 1939—the very month Evie turned 10 years old—Evie left Germany on a train headed for France. From there she took a ferry to Harwich, England, where she was met by two Quaker women. On September 1, 1939, Hitler invaded Poland; two days later, England declared war on Germany. England's borders were now closed to German immigrants.

Otto could no longer join Evie. Evie settled in with her foster family, the Whyatts, who lived in Ipswich, a small village about an hour from London.

Gilbert Whyatt, a manager in a manufacturing company, and his wife, Irene, had two children, Philip and Lois, both of whom were about Evie's age. They played with Evie right away and made her feel welcome. Mr. Whyatt gave Evie an hour's lesson in English every day, a gesture which Evie appreciated even then.

"I wanted to be assimilated," she recalls. "I wanted to be the same. I wanted to fit in and be accepted."

Through the Red Cross, Evie and her father

*Eveliese Shuermann was only 9 years old when a classmate come up to her
and yelled, "Your father's a dirty Jew! Your father's a dirty Jew!"*

managed to exchange one bland letter a month, consisting of only 25 words or less, since all mail going to England was read and censored by German officials. But at least Evie knew that her father was alive.

Then one day the letters stopped. No explanation, no news. Her foster parents tried to be comforting and told her to be hopeful. Evie tried not to grieve, even though her mother had died only a short time ago and now her father had disappeared.

"I just had to stuff everything," she says. "I totally lost touch with my German roots and was raised as a stoic English girl."

When families were evacuated from Ipswich to protect them from German bombing, Irene Whyatt and the children moved to Morecambe, a small town in Lancashire, where Irene's mother had a house. Irene and the children lived there for two years; Mr. Whyatt visited on weekends. As the RAF sent bombing missions to Germany in retaliation for the air raids on England, the people around Evie all cheered. But Evie didn't know how to respond: Did she belong to Germany or England? Germany was persecuting the Jews, and this had forced her to leave. But should

she cheer for England while her father and other relatives were trapped in Germany and, therefore, in danger of being killed by English bombs?

Trying to Conform

IN ENGLAND EVIE FELT OTHER STRESSES AS well. Her natural father had warned her to behave and follow the rules in England: Always say "please" and "thank you." She was fearful that one wrong move would cause her foster parents to abandon her. So, despite the fact that the Whyatts were extremely welcoming, Evie felt a constant pressure to live up to expectations that she hadn't been raised with: Simple things—like using the proper British manners while dining—took on added weight. Evie now felt totally dependent upon the kindness of her foster family.

Even the informal geography quizzes that Mr. Whyatt would hold over meals took on great significance: With each wrong answer, Evie felt that she would be in jeopardy. Evie had been raised in a family where she had been doted upon; both of her parents had been openly affectionate with her. The

Whyatts were kind and fair, but they were typically British, reserved with their emotions. Sometimes Evie mistook their coolness as a sign of disapproval, not realizing that they were naturally reticent.

When Evie turned 16, the British government tried to put her in a detention camp for "enemy aliens": Evie was still a German citizen, and now old enough to be treated as an adult. But Mr. Whyatt refused to allow the government to take this action, arguing that by this time she was now part of the family. He won the fight—but Evie didn't find out that he had advocated for her until years later.

A Letter Arrives

ON MAY 7, 1945, THE WAR IN EUROPE ENDED. Soon after, Evie received a letter from her father. Miraculously, he was alive; he had hidden in the countryside with a German Jewish woman named Hanny Geese and her *mischling* child, Heinz. (Hanny's husband, a Christian musician with a German orchestra, had divorced Hanny when his employer threatened to fire him if he remained married to a Jewish woman.) Otto had managed to obtain false documents and he had been working incognito on a farm owned by Nazis.

Excited to receive her father's letter, Evie made plans to meet him in Bonn, Germany, where Otto and Hanny had resettled. Evie knew that she was in-credibly lucky; most children who left Germany on *Kindertransports* never saw their parents again. But it was not until November 1947 that she was able to get the proper travel documents. When she arrived, their reunion was unexpectedly painful: Evie had been living with the Whyatts for almost nine years and she was an integral part of their family. Now 18, she was a young woman, but her father couldn't grasp that she had grown up; he wanted to hold her on his lap, as if she were still a child.

"He still thought of me as a little girl," recalls Evie. "I felt almost as though he were a stranger. I still loved him, but I felt guilty that I didn't feel the same way he did. I was torn."

They spent six weeks together, talking and traveling to the countryside and revisiting Evie's home town. Otto wanted Evie to remain with him in post-war Germany, even though the country was in shambles: There was little electricity and a severe shortage of food and housing. People could get water only from pumps. Jobs were scarce. Despite these hardships, Evie's father still had a strong sense of loyalty to Germany and wanted to stay there. Evie wanted to live with her father, but she could not live in Germany.

They finally compromised: Evie's father offered to emigrate to Chicago to join his brother, Willy, and his family, who had settled there before the war.

Once again Evie had to say good-bye to her family, only this time it was her foster family, the family she had lived with during her formative teenage years. She was once again torn and distrustful: "I am never going to love anybody again," she remembers saying. She swore that she would never allow herself to form a deep tie again.

Top, left to right: Evie and her mother's family, who eventually shunned her; Evie (right) and her friend Maria (left), with Evie's mother and father, 1936; Evie and her mother, 1938.

"It's taken me a whole lifetime to figure out who I am," says Evie. "I spent so much time trying to fit in or be what I thought other people wanted me to be, I was like a chameleon all this time. And I'm still trying to resolve my identity."

Voyage to America

IN 1948 EVIE BOARDED A SHIP BOUND FOR America. (Her father would follow soon after.) On the ship, her life once again changed: She met a young man named Ray Jacobson, a young American Lutheran of Swedish descent. Ray had been studying in a university in Stockholm on a GI Bill. He was traveling back to his home in Minneapolis. On the ship Evie and Ray spent several hours together and Ray asked if he could write to her, to find out how she was adapting to her new life in America.

When Evie arrived in Chicago, more troubles confronted her: She ran up to hug and kiss her cousin. His wife exclaimed, "We don't do that in this country!"

Evie felt the same nervousness she had experienced when she had arrived in England: Behave or you could be out on the street. Become whom you think people want you to be in order to survive.

A year later her father, then 60 years old, arrived from Germany with Hanny. When he did, the pressure on Evie intensified. "I wasn't comfortable with him," she says. "He wanted me to spend time with

him—maybe more than I wanted to. I had this feeling of guilt if I didn't measure up to what he wanted."

She got a job working in a garment sweatshop to help pay the bills. She also continued writing to Ray Jacobson, and through their letters they fell in love. He proposed on December 31, 1949. Evie, almost 21, accepted. They married the following August. Since Ray was working as an engineer with a large company in Minneapolis, he asked Evie to join him there. Evie agreed, even though she felt guilty about leaving her father in Chicago, particularly since he was having such a hard time there adjusting to American life.

In Chicago, Otto and Hanny married, but Otto could not find a job; so he walked from door to door selling can openers to earn money, longing to be back in Germany. Despite Hitler's terrible policies toward the Jews, he still considered Germany his homeland; there he could speak the language and work in his given profession. At least, that is what he thought.

Evie also found adjusting to life in Minneapolis more difficult than she had anticipated. On top of the normal stresses of living in a new city, Evie was racked with guilt and ambivalence, torn between her love for her new husband and her sense of obligation to be with her father, who had settled in America to be with her. Was her loyalty to her husband, Ray, or her father, Otto?

The following year she gave birth to her first daughter, Pam, and these stresses escalated. Evie fell into a serious depression and sought help and guidance from a therapist. To heal the wounds with her father, she made frequent trips to Chicago to visit him and Hanny. But it wasn't until 1957 that she and her father developed a real closeness. Then Otto died unexpectedly the following year from a lingering heart ailment.

In 1966 Ray was transferred to Rochester. Evie, now the mother of two teenage daughters, took a part-time job as a teller in a bank. Some customers would assume she was Jewish because of her last name—Jacobson—which was a common German/Jewish name. She would always point out that her husband was of Swedish descent.

"I felt that I was denying my heritage," she explains, "but I was afraid of what people would think if they knew that I was partly Jewish. Some of my co-workers would make snide remarks about Jewish customers." For many years, Evie would say nothing when she heard these remarks; after all, antisemitism had ruined her life once. She did not want to suffer from it again. Finally, after working in the bank for ten years, she decided to confront her co-workers, telling them their remarks were racist and that she, in fact, was of Jewish heritage.

"I was scared," she says. "I was really shaking inside. But I decided I couldn't be quiet anymore."

Once she confronted them, she found new strength from simply telling the truth. "It made me feel more empowered," she says. "I was not hiding something about myself anymore." Evie began making connections with other Holocaust survivors in her area; soon she felt strong enough to share her story with schoolchildren in Rochester.

Chameleon No More

EVIE JACOBSON'S STORY IS ONE MORE example of the way in which the Nazis partly succeeded in stripping human beings of their humanity and their identity.

"It's taken me a whole lifetime to figure out who I am," says Evie today. "I spent so much time trying to fit in or be what I thought other people wanted me to be, I was like a chameleon all this time. And I'm still trying to resolve my identity."

Evie told her two daughters, Pam and Debbie, about her mixed heritage when they were small children: She wanted them to know that they had a Jewish grandfather. But she was not willing or able to talk about her past with others. Eventually, with the help of therapists, friends, and family, she gathered the strength and understanding to do so, overcoming learned habits of silence and suppression.

"It was just always something she talked about, at whatever level we could understand," says her older daughter, Pam Barnes, 49, a mother and special-education teacher, who lives in Vermont with her husband and three children. "It's in her nature not to stuff things, to always look for answers and share things with people in her life."

Evie's younger daughter, Debbie, 46, is also close to her mother and sees her parents often. Debbie lives in Rochester, where she is the director of public relations for the Rochester Museum and Science Center.

In deference to her husband, Ray, Evie joined a

Lutheran church in Minneapolis, but she was never a devout Christian and raised both of her children to be open-minded about religion. Spirituality, however, is increasingly important to Evie; although she does not embrace any organized religion, the philosophies of Unitarianism and Buddhism appeal to her. She has also begun painting mystical watercolors to express her inner beliefs.

Evie has told her grandchildren about her Jewish father, and they are proud of the association. Just a few years ago, Evie's grandson, Michael, and her granddaughter Lisa, completed high school projects based on the journal that Otto kept while he was in hiding in Germany; her granddaughter Kathryn used Evie's story to illustrate an immigration project in fourth grade.

Evie has also been deeply touched by her foster family. Many years after the war ended, the German government offered large sums of money to the families who took in *Kindertransport* children as recompense for taking care of its citizens. The Whyatts refused the money, saying that they had raised Evie as a member of their family: They did not expect to be paid for it. The gesture hit home.

"They had me for nine years—I was part of the family," says Evie. "It's unbelievable that anyone would do that." ✡

Evie and Ray Jacobson outside their Rochester home.

Excerpt from Otto Shuermann's diary about his reunion with Evie after nine years of separation.

Here in Bonn I received the first letter from my child. It was an intensely powerful experience for me...to learn that my child was all right and that she was living with the Whyatt family, that she had been treated like one of their own children, was healthy, felt happy, and was overjoyed to know that I am still alive.

After New Year's, we took a trip to Hildesheim and Pattensen. Eveliese was very shocked at the ruins of the city, and here in Hildesheim...she recognized places where she was happy, places where she played, and asked about names of her little girlfriends. We took a side-trip to Pattensen. She was horrified at the condition of the Jewish cemetery and she expressed her anger with the words, "I don't believe I could live any longer in this Germany."

Teacher illustrating the physiognomy of the "Aryan" ideal to a group of students.

Race Science

Teaching Lies

According to Nazi doctrine, true "Aryans" had blond hair, blue eyes, fair skin, and muscular torsos. They were handsome, Nordic-looking people. Jews, in contrast, were ugly and slothful-looking. They had black, curly hair, large, bulbous noses, large bellies, menacing eyes, and "distinctive" left ears, which is why all German Jews were photographed for their identity cards with their left ears exposed. To promote this stereotype, teachers were required to teach "race science" to their pupils; the state supplied them with charts and graphs to do so.

Of course, these doctrines were utterly ridiculous; many "pure-bred" Germans looked nothing at all like the Aryan ideal. Many had brown hair and brown eyes. Not all Nazis were blond and blue-eyed. (Hitler himself and his chief henchmen, Goebbels, Göring, Eichmann, and Himmler, were dark-haired and hardly handsome!) Ironically, many Jews were blond and fair-skinned and looked more like the stereotypical "Aryan" than the Germans did. Rosemarie Molser, Ellen Arndt, Evie Jacobson, Lily Haber, and Bill Braun were all blond, slim, and extremely good-looking. As a young child, Rosemarie was called to the front of the class, where her teacher used her to exemplify the "ideal" Aryan girl.

The Nazis could never explain these contradictions; instead, they ignored reality and continued to persecute Jews. B.L.

Profile No. 5

A Harrowing Journey: From Germany to India
The Story of Nathan Taylor

BY PATTI SINGER

How the Teichlers, forced out of Germany, escaped to Poland with the help of smugglers, survived a rebellion in Iraq, rafted down the Tigris, drove through the desert to Palestine in an old Mercedes, and finally settled in Bombay, India, for four years.

AMERICA MAY BE THE LAND OF MILK AND honey, but for one 15-year-old German-Jewish boy who escaped the Holocaust, it was the land of cornflakes and Coca Cola. Nathan Siegfried Teichler, a retired pathologist who changed his name to Taylor, arrived in the United States in 1946 aboard the SS *Battle Creek Victory*. The ship was named after the Michigan city that invented cornflakes, and the sailors on board introduced the young boy to Coca-Cola. The five-week voyage was the last leg of an eight-year journey that Nathan and his parents made

to escape the Nazis, a journey that took them to Trieste, Italy; Istanbul, Turkey; Baghdad, Iraq; and, finally, to Calcutta, India.

When Nathan Siegfried Teichler was a second-grader in his hometown, Erfurt, Germany, all his classmates became members of the Hitler Youth. They got red armbands with black swastikas, brown short pants, and brown short-sleeve shirts. All the children except Nathan. It was 1937, four years after Hitler had become Chancellor of Germany.

"The teachers knew that I was Jewish, and so I did

Top: Nathan and his parents in India during the summer of 1944. They arrived in India in summer 1941 and lived there until the war ended. Opposite page: Nathan and his mother, 1931.

not get a uniform," recalls Nathan. "Later, they had a big festival and all the kids put on their uniforms and marched outside, carrying flags and singing songs. And I couldn't take part. It was frightening to watch the kids march, because I knew they were up to no good. People don't usually march with flags and use the goose step."

But when Nathan asked his teacher why he couldn't participate, the teacher sent him home, saying, "Don't pay any attention to it. Just go home. You don't have to do any work today." When Nathan asked his parents, they were equally vague.

Nathan, an only child, lived with his mother, Bertha, and his father, Jakob, a wine salesman, on the outskirts of Erfurt, a small town in central Germany. The family lived in a large, concrete apartment building surrounded by fields. Jakob and Bertha Teichler had lived in Germany since they were teenagers. However, since they had been born in Galicia, Poland, the German government considered them Polish citizens. Even Nathan was considered Polish since children took on their father's citizenship.

Yet the Teichlers thought of themselves as German. They rarely went to synagogue and had little contact with other Jewish families. Even Nathan's name, Siegfried, reflected a German identity. His parents, who had named him Nathan Solomon after his great-grandfather, thought one Jewish name was enough, so they had "Solomon" changed to "Siegfried."

Soon after Hitler came to power in 1933, Jakob moved the family to Holland to avoid the Nazi restrictions. But Jakob couldn't learn the Dutch language and couldn't find a job. When his money ran out, he contacted his old employers in Germany, who invited him to return. They assured him that the Nazis

posed no threat and that he would be safe working for non-Jews. But when the Teichlers returned, they found themselves increasingly excluded from German life. Nathan felt shunned by his classmates and the neighborhood children.

By March 1938 Jakob, by law no longer able to work for the wine company, was fired, since German companies were no longer allowed to hire Jews. Jakob and Bertha decided to join Bertha's parents in Berlin, where they thought there would be less antisemitism.

Berlin—the "Safer City"

FORTUNATELY, BERTHA'S PARENTS, JOSEF and Regina Spindel, lived in a ten-room apartment. Several of Bertha's siblings were also living there when Nathan and his parents arrived. At first it seemed like a holiday for the small child. But as the days rolled into weeks, Nathan began to feel that this was his new home.

Bertha enrolled Nathan, now 7 years old, in a Jewish school, Adass Yisroel. But he made few friends there. "They considered me an outsider," he recalls, "because I was neither a Berliner nor identified with the Jewish community."

Although Nathan learned to accept his Jewish identity, he didn't really know what it meant. And he came to resent it, because being Jewish was also becoming dangerous. "My teacher said to me, 'If you don't wear your *yarmulke* [a Jewish skullcap] outside in the open sky, God will be angry with you.' But I knew that if I wore it, the Nazi hoodlums would come after me. I figured they were more dangerous than God; I figured God would understand."

As antisemitic restrictions increased, Nathan's world grew smaller

"My teacher said to me, 'If you don't wear your yarmulke [a Jewish skullcap] outside in the open sky, God will be angry with you.' But I knew that if I wore it, the Nazi hoodlums would come after me. I figured they were more dangerous than God; I figured God would understand."

and lonelier. The isolation didn't come only from strangers; his parents refused to answer his questions about why the men in the streets were wearing brown shirts or black uniforms. Instead of telling him what was happening, they told him not to wander far from home. They tried to protect Nathan.

Early in November 1938, a week before *Kristallnacht*, Nathan was awakened by a loud banging on the family's apartment door. Armed German soldiers had come to pick up Jakob.

"You're going to Poland," they charged. "You're not a German citizen. Pack your belongings and come with us."

Jakob, who secretly carried his money on a belt inside his clothing, packed very little. Then he was put onto a truck while Bertha and Nathan watched in shock. At the Polish border, Jakob was abandoned. But he managed to walk about five miles to a train station, where he bought a ticket for Krakow, a city in Poland where German was spoken.

After Jakob left, Bertha tried to restore an environment of normality—a normality that collapsed on November 9, when Nazi hoodlums swept through Berlin, smashing store windows, burning synagogues, and arresting more than 30,000 Jewish men. The vandalism took place far away from Nathan's home,

but it didn't matter: The Nazis had already shattered the life of his family.

After the *Kristallnacht* pogrom, Bertha kept Nathan at home, allowing him to leave the apartment only to attend school. Six months later, she received a letter from Jakob instructing her to take Nathan to an apartment in Breslau, a city in eastern Germany about forty miles from the Polish border. There, smugglers hired by Jakob would take Bertha and Nathan across the border. Even though the Germans considered them Polish citizens, the Polish government wouldn't take back Polish-born German Jews who had let their citizenship lapse.

In the Hands of Smugglers

ON MAY 2, BERTHA AND NATHAN ARRIVED at a small, shabby apartment in Breslau where three hired smugglers were waiting. Nathan was frightened of the men, and that night he slept in a bed with Bertha. When he awoke the next morning and saw that he was safe, he felt better.

Later that day the smugglers drove them to a large corridor of barren land—about one mile wide—that separated Poland and Germany and belonged to neither country. Guards were positioned at each

Top: Nathan on the first day of school holding a *Zuckertüte*, a cone filled with candy, that all German schoolchildren received.

border. The smugglers deliberately chose May 3 because it was Polish Independence Day and they figured the Polish patrols—whom they needed to pass to get into Poland—would be drunk by evening, when they hoped to cross.

First, however, they had to sneak past the German guards, who were not supposed to let people through unless they had exit papers. Neither Bertha nor Nathan had any. As they approached the border, a woman unexpectedly stepped out of a wooden hut.

"She examined us very carefully," recalls Nathan. "She opened our suitcases. She searched us to see if we were carrying any weapons. She was very nice, very friendly. 'Be careful,' she warned us. 'The guards are nearby. Go down the hill. When you see a stream, crawl low.' She told us exactly how to avoid detection from the Poles, because the Poles didn't want to have the problem of arresting us and sending us back to Germany."

As Nathan and Bertha came to the brook, it shimmered brightly, lit up by a full moon, making crossing dangerous. "It looked very scary to me," recalls Nathan, who was only 8 years old. "For the first time, I realized that this was bad business. We had no papers. If they arrested us, we would be sent back to Germany. I was frozen with the cold and with fear. I hoped for the best."

After crossing the shining stream, the smugglers guided them quietly into the woods. The Polish guards were several hundred yards away, up on a hill. Nathan could hear their drunken shouts and laughter. Soon Bertha and Nathan were met by a second group of smugglers, who took them to a waiting car and drove them over the Polish border to Katowicze, a small city near Auschwitz, where a deadly concentration camp would be established. From Katowicze, Bertha and Nathan boarded a train for Krakow.

"We were totally alone, and sat in the train until dawn," Nathan recalls. "When the train finally started,

Hitler Youth

When Nathan was a second-grader in Erfurt, Germany, all his classmates were members of the Hitler Youth. They wore uniforms similar to those pictured above—brown short pants, brown short-sleeve shirts, special neckties, and red armbands with black swastikas. They belonged to groups that sponsored trips, activities, and sporting events and prepared them to be loyal Nazis.

*Nathan's mother traveled to Berlin, and bribed a German officer into giving her
a handwritten exit permit. It cost her most of her husband's severance pay.*

the trip took only two hours at the very most. In Krakow my father met us at the railway station." Seeing his father filled Nathan with relief.

No Welcome in Poland

JAKOB LIVED IN A TWO-BEDROOM APARTment on the outskirts of Krakow, only a streetcar ride to town. But no one ventured out very far. Jakob did not remember how to speak Polish, and he couldn't find a job. He spent his days hanging out with other German deportees in cafés. When Nathan went outside, kids threw rocks at him, and tormented him. They knew, from his halting Polish and his fine clothes, that he wasn't one of them. To protect him from more abuse, Bertha did not enroll Nathan in school; instead, he stayed home, reading the same books over and over, playing with a stamp album, and complaining to his parents.

On September 1, 1939, the Germans invaded Poland. Stories spread that the Germans were arrest-

ing Poles and Jews. Men in Jakob's apartment building were planning to hide in the woods. They invited Jakob to join them. Jakob agreed, but when he met with them the following evening, he said, "Wait!" He'd forgotten his toothbrush. "Are you crazy?" the men said. "Do you realize that where we're going, you're not going to be able to brush your teeth?" But Jakob stubbornly ran back to get his toothbrush. When he returned, the men had left. He found out later that they were captured outside of Krakow; half were killed, the others were tortured. "If my father had gone with them, he would have never returned," sums up Nathan. "And that is how a toothbrush saved our lives."

Jakob now knew they had to leave Poland. Jews were being segregated and had to wear a yellow star on their clothing to identify them as Jews. In order to leave Poland, the Teichlers tried to get an exit permit from the German government. In February 1940, Bertha traveled to Berlin, where she had the name from smugglers of a German officer she could bribe

Top, left to right: Passport photos of Nathan, Bertha, and Jakob, spring 1941.

to obtain a handwritten exit permit. It cost her most of her husband's severance pay. Next she paid a forger to prepare false passports.

In March 1940 the Teichler family left Poland, hoping to get to America. Their odyssey began with a train trip from Krakow to Trieste, Italy, where Jakob thought it might be easier to get a ship to America, since not many refugees took this route.

But they missed their connections to Trieste and spent the night in Vienna. The next day they boarded a train to Italy. Knowing that Austrian officials would inspect their baggage, the Teichlers were prepared with a bribe. Since German Jews could take only 10 marks (the equivalent of a couple of dollars) across the German border, many Jews used their valuables—their furs and jewelry—as bribes. Nathan's parents had none of these. But they had something else.

A Rare Stamp Collection

NATHAN HAD STARTED COLLECTING stamps in Germany. By the time the Teichlers left Poland, he had accumulated many German stamps, as well as some special editions in honor of a heroic Polish general named Pilsudski. When Bertha packed their suitcases for the trip, she put Nathan's stamp album on the top of their belongings in the first suitcase. The inspector came by, opened the suitcase, and saw the album. "His eyes widened," recalls Nathan. "He said, 'I'm not sure if you can bring this across the border. I have to ask my superior.' Then he took the stamp album and disappeared. He never showed up again.

"I became angrier and angrier about losing the album, and then I felt the train moving," recalls Nathan. "I was too young to understand that it was a good thing he had taken the stamps, because if the inspector had searched through the cases, he would have taken other things that we needed."

Underneath his coat, Nathan was wearing six watches on his arms. In Trieste, Jakob sold the watches for cash. They lived on the money for the next three months, while they tried to get papers to leave. In the meantime, Nathan went to school, and, for the first time in many years, he had friends. "We'd go to the piazza and hang around the orange carts, where vendors would give us fruit, because they knew we children had no money," he recalls. "We would also go every day to the harbor and watch the big ocean liners, hoping to leave on one of them." But the U.S. consul would not give his family entry papers.

When Mussolini, the Fascist ruler of Italy, allied himself officially with Hitler on June 10, 1940, the Teichlers realized that it was dangerous to stay in Italy. Despairing of getting visas to the U.S., they decided to travel east and took a train to Istanbul, where they thought they would be safe. In Istanbul, Jakob met some well-to-do French Jews who arranged for him to work as a lingerie salesman while he tried to find passage on a ship to America. The Teichlers decided to travel to Shanghai, since it was the closest major port that was not occupied by Germans. But since the Mediterranean was filled with German submarines, they decided to travel to Shanghai by train.

Saved by a Sheik

IN THE SPRING OF 1941, BERTHA AND JAKOB joined twenty other Jewish refugees, all of whom intended to take a train to Diyarbakir in eastern Turkey. From there, they planned to bribe their way through Syria and into Baghdad, where they could take a train to Shanghai. But French officials refused to let the group board the train. Since the roads were impassable due to a spring runoff, they hired Kurdish natives to take them down the Tigris on a raft made of wooden planks lashed to buoyant sheepskins.

"The first night, we were in a big hurry to get to

Iraq," recalls Nathan. "But the Kurds told us to stop. It was only 4 p.m. We said no. So we continued and, as the sun set, we hit some rocks. The raft started to list. The women started to scream. Fortunately, nobody fell overboard into the freezing-cold water."

When they reached shore, the group had to walk about three miles to the nearest village in the pitch dark. Their journey to Iraq wound up taking almost two weeks. Each night, they stayed in a different village, where they slept on thick carpets on the ground. "When we got to Iraq there was a gorge and there were hot springs," recalls Nathan.

"We stopped at the hot springs and bathed. But we slept in the caves overnight with the donkeys. I was allowed to ride the donkeys. That was the greatest thrill of my life. I'd never ridden an animal in my life, and I was on a donkey. My parents were appalled because fleas bit us. This didn't bother me."

In April 1941 the Teichlers arrived in Baghdad in the midst of an uprising: Natives were attacking the British, who governed there. Jakob wanted to leave as soon as possible and hired two smugglers, a Palestinian and a Lebanese, to drive the family across the desert to Haifa. The family piled into an old Mercedes-Benz with windows so scratched and sunbleached that Nathan could barely see the sand as they drove from Baghdad to Palestine.

When they arrived, the British—who were in charge of Palestine—would not let the Teichlers enter, since there were stiff quotas on how many Jews could

emigrate there. The Teichlers drove back to Iraq, where there was now violent fighting in the streets. The mob had taken over. They were murdering young non-Arabic women and dragging their bodies through the main street. Jakob found refuge in a cheap hotel where a sheik was living. When Arab terrorists broke into their hotel, the sheik protected them.

"If anything happened to us, he thought Allah would hold him responsible," recalls Nathan with a smile. "So his guards threw out the Arab mob and locked the doors. And we were safe."

From there Jakob moved the family to the large Iraqi port city of Basra. They sweated out July, trying to find available ship tickets. Then they heard that a secretary to a British consul was hosting a dinner where he would secretly be selling tickets to refugees for passage to India. India would get them closer to Shanghai and out of Iraq.

At the lavish party, Jakob gave all his money to the secretary, in exchange for a plain envelope that was supposed to contain vouchers for tickets. When Jakob arrived at the dock, the clerk said the vouchers were worthless. Jakob refused to believe he had been scammed; he began arguing loudly. Then Bertha joined in, creating such a ruckus that the ship's captain came over. When Bertha explained that they had been swindled, the captain phoned the official and threatened to have him fired if he did not deliver proper tickets. Apparently, the secretary had performed the ruse often with other naïve refugees.

Top: Nathan's parents, safe in the Bronx in New York City, 1947.

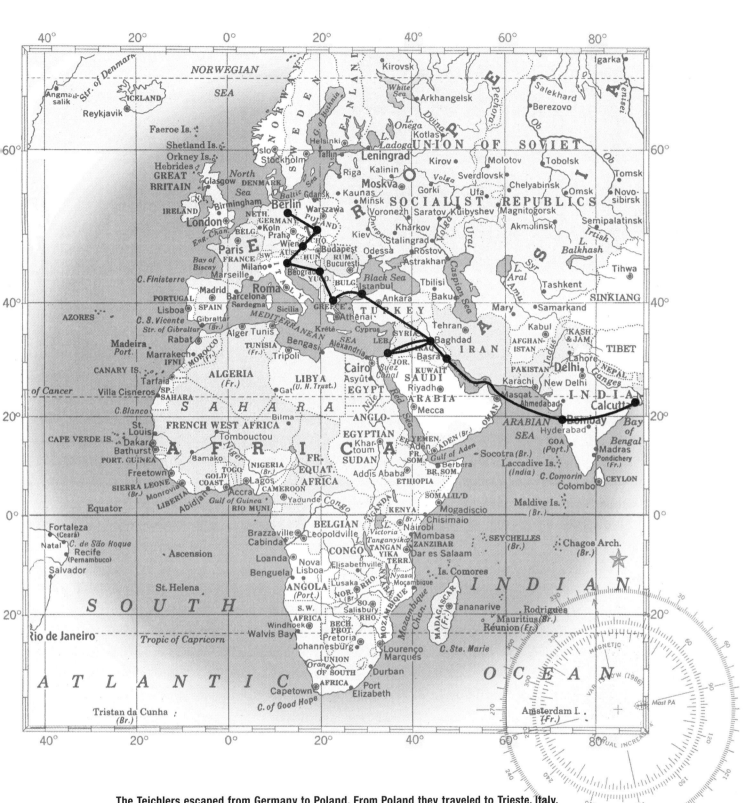

The Teichlers escaped from Germany to Poland. From Poland they traveled to Trieste, Italy.
From Trieste they headed east to Istanbul, Turkey; then traveled on a raft down the Tigris to Baghdad,
in the middle of an uprising. They drove to Palestine—and had to return. Finally, they made it to Basra,
an Iraqi port city; from Basra they sailed to Bombay, India, where they lived until the war ended.

Passage to India

WHEN THE TEICHLERS AT LAST SAILED from the harbor, there were only a few passengers on their huge ship. Later, they found out why: It was loaded with munitions. Nonetheless, they arrived in Bombay safely, with almost no money in their pockets. A Jewish relief association that fed and housed refugees, put them up in a huge Quonset hut with hundreds of cots. It was July 1941. They were starting over again, for the fifth time in three years.

Bertha began working as a masseuse, even though she had no training at all. With money wired to them from Bertha's brother, Max, who had emigrated to America, they found an apartment. Bombay was so bug-ridden that Jakob decided to sell insecticide. He got a formula from his brother-in-law, Ferdinand, who was in Palestine. Then he formed a partnership with a Polish lawyer he had met in Bombay. The insecticide sold well; Jakob moved the family to a larger apartment and hired a servant. Nathan enrolled in a Jesuit academy where a ruddy-faced, chain-smoking priest took him under his wing. Nathan played cricket and ran track. He also formed a close friendship with a Jewish classmate, Ellis Meyer, who filled a void in his life.

When the war ended in 1945, the end of the Teichlers' long journey seemed in sight. Uncle Max sent affidavits so they could obtain U.S. visas. But once again they faced obstacles. The only ships leaving Bombay were military carriers; they wouldn't accept passengers. So Jakob took the family to Calcutta, which had a larger port and more ships. On the lengthy train ride, Bertha became very ill; they had to wait a month in Calcutta while she recovered. They finally boarded the SS *Battle Creek Victory*, a large naval ship. Three days into their voyage, passengers learned the ship was carrying dismantled warheads.

The Teichlers had hoped to arrive in New York City, where Uncle Max was waiting. But since the ship was carrying explosives, it was diverted to Charleston, South Carolina. After disembarking, the Teichlers took a taxi to Union Station, where they could board a train to New York City. Driving to the station, they saw little huts that looked as though they were made out of tin cans.

At Union Station, Nathan saw two gates: One was marked *White*. The other bore a sign, *Colored*. Nathan asked the conductor what the signs meant.

His eight-year journey from oppression to freedom held one last lesson in discrimination.

Nathan and his family remained in New York City. Eventually, Nathan received an M.D. from Columbia University's College of Physicians and Surgeons. He did an internship at Strong Memorial Hospital in Rochester. Then he moved to Boston and later Syracuse to practice medicine.

In 1967 he moved back to Rochester to join the Rochester General Hospital as a pathologist. He married and had four children. He is now married to Alisa Cook. ✡

Top: Nathan Taylor at home.

THE
Polish Expulsion

Stranded in No Man's Land

On October 27, 1938, German police began expelling Polish-born Jews, like Nathan's father, Jakob Teichler, who lived in Germany. The expulsion was a response to a decree issued by Poland requiring all Polish citizens living abroad to revalidate their passports by October 29—or lose the right to return to Poland. Although many Polish-born Jews had lived in Germany for decades, the Third Reich refused to grant them German citizenship. The Nazis did not want Polish-born Jews to live in Germany permanently.

So, the Germans acted preemptively and expelled Polish expatriates without warning. Often using force, they rounded up 17,000 Polish-born Jews—most of them men—and deported them by train to the Polish border towns of Zbaszyn and Beuthen. Polish authorities, surprised by the action, tried to keep the refugees in these towns while they negotiated with Germany to take them back.

In Zbaszyn the refugees found shelter in the stables of a military riding school and in a flour mill owned by a local Jew. Others found rooms in private homes. Meanwhile, the Joint Distribution Committee organized a full-fledged refugee camp with cultural and medical facilities, where Jews could live temporarily.

On January 24, 1939, refugees were allowed to return to Germany to settle their affairs. But they had to deposit all their earnings from property settlements into blocked bank accounts, accessible only to German officials. In August the Zbaszyn refugee camp was closed. Less than a month later, German troops invaded Poland. Jews were again rounded up, only this time they were confined in ghettos, and eventually deported to concentration camps.   B.L.

Top, left to right: Refugees peeling potatoes in Zbaszyn refugee camp; Refugees temporarily sheltered in military riding school.

Sanctuary in Shanghai:

The Story of Hermann Goldfarb

ADAPTED FROM HIS MEMOIR

Hermann Goldfarb's parents fled to Argentina from Munich in 1924. But life in the new country was so hard that they returned to Germany. Later the family left Germany again; this time they were split apart. Hermann traveled to Shanghai on his own, to join a small but thriving community of Jewish refugees.

HERMANN GOLDFARB WAS BORN IN MUnich, Germany, in 1919. His parents had emigrated there from the Austro-Hungarian empire in the early 1900's. In 1923, the youthful Adolf Hitler tried to overthrow the German government in Munich in a revolt known as the "beer hall putsch." Fearing for their safety, Hermann's parents, Selig and Miriam, sold most of their belongings and emigrated to Argentina.

Upon arrival, Selig received a small piece of land and a small house from the Jewish Colonization Enterprise, an organization that encouraged such emigration. But the house was extremely primitive and the land too small to cultivate. So Hermann's father got a horse and buggy and began selling items to farmers in the area. When Selig began suffering from severe asthma attacks, Miriam finally convinced him that this was not the right place to raise children.

In 1925, the family sailed back to Europe to join Helene, Miriam's sister, who was living in Chrzanow, Poland. Hermann's brother, Eric, was born there in 1925. The next year, the Goldfarbs moved to Berlin, where Selig had found a job as a salesman. Hermann was enrolled in a boys' school run by the Jewish community; his younger sister, Sonja, also started school.

"When Hitler became Chancellor in 1933, life for

Top: Hermann and Else Goldfarb, Shanghai, 1946. Opposite page: Hermann and Else with their daughter, Helen, Shanghai, 1947.

us changed even more dramatically," Hermann says. "We lived in constant fear. Jews were beaten, and some were picked up on the streets and disappeared. They were never seen or heard from again."

In 1934, Hermann graduated from high school and became an apprentice in cabinetmaking at the Rudolf Klein furniture factory in Berlin, an old, established firm owned by a Hungarian Jew. Soon after that, Hermann's father died, at the age of 55. The family had to move to another apartment. "My mother tried hard to get us out of Germany while there was still time," Hermann says. "But no country was willing to accept a widow with three children."

"Nowhere to Go!"

IN LATE OCTOBER 1938, HERMANN WAS AT work as usual when he was called to the phone. "It was my mother telling me that the police were looking for me," he says.

He was the victim of a grim Catch-22. "German officials were rounding up all Jews born in Poland and sending them to a barren strip of land between Poland and Germany," he says. "Even though my parents had lived in Germany since 1902, the Austro-Hungarian area where they were born had become part of Poland after World War I. The German government considered us to be Polish citizens. Even though I was born, raised, and educated in Germany, the German government considered me a Polish citizen since children took on the citizenship of their fathers. They were looking for me to expel me to Poland.

"My mother told me to go

into hiding until the action was called off. I left work immediately and stayed for two weeks with friends. Luckily I was still in hiding during *Kristallnacht*, which occurred less than two weeks later. It was the beginning of the horrors that would follow."

When Hermann emerged from his hiding place, he went back to work. The following March 28, 1939, he received a letter from the police, ordering him to leave Germany within 24 hours. "It was impossible," Hermann declares. "Nowhere to go!

"I went to the police and tried to get an extension. When it was granted, I tried to get a permit to enter England with the help of my Zionist youth group, but they couldn't do anything for me. On June 15, I received another letter from the police, informing me that I had until June 30 to leave or I would be arrested. I knew what that meant.

"My mother and I went to all the organizations that were supposed to assist us—without any results. Then, at a meeting of a Jewish woman's organization, she met a woman who promised to help: She had booked passage on a Japanese ship going to Shanghai, China, and she was willing to give her ticket to me. The woman had connections with the travel agency and could get another ticket for herself a month later.

"Since China was one of the few countries that Jews could enter without any immigration papers, many were trying to go. But all the passages were sold out. I was very fortunate to be offered a ticket; I accepted it. The Japanese ship was scheduled to leave from Naples, Italy, on July 2. I had only eight days to take care of all the formalities and pack, but by June 29 I was ready to go. My mother and my younger brother, Eric, took me to the train station in Berlin, where I boarded the train for Rome and Naples. I was 19 years old and did not know when—or if—I would ever see my family again."

As the train headed toward the Italian border, all the passengers were afraid of what might happen. "There officials checked our passports," Hermann recalls. "Then the customs officials arrived: 'Are there any Jews here?' they asked. We had to get off the train. They conducted a strip search on us and also searched our suitcases. By the time they finished, we had missed the train to Rome. But we managed to catch the next one, and crossed the border into Italy! I had left Germany on time! My sister and brother also got out. Sonja went to England; Eric went to a children's home in France on a *Kindertransport*."

Life in an Alien City

I N ROME HERMANN CHANGED TRAINS FOR Naples. The next day he boarded a 10,500-ton ship, the *Hakozaki Maru*, a combination freighter and passenger ship carrying about 80 passengers, most of them German refugees. They sailed to Port Said, where they entered the Suez Canal; it took twelve hours for the ship to get through the canal. On July 22 they reached Singapore; six days later they passed Hong Kong. On July 31—after sailing for almost a month—Hermann reached Shanghai.

Shanghai, then a city of about four million inhabitants, is located in the Yangtze River delta and is one of the world's greatest seaports. But the city was overcrowded and filled with unsanitary quarters. Even so, many refugees fled there because they didn't need visas or any other papers to enter.

"We arrived at the Shanghai-Hongkew Wharf,

and from the dock I could see tall and beautiful buildings along the Bund, the famous street that lines the waterfront," Hermann remembers. "I was assigned to stay in Pingliang Road Camp for single men, which had been a cement-block factory. As I walked through strange and dirty streets, carrying a small suitcase and wearing a suit that was too heavy for the hot weather, many Chinese stared at me. By the time I arrived, my clothes were wet from sweat.

"About twenty young men welcomed me. Inside, there was a large hall with 200 bunk beds, as well as a washroom and showers. The toilet was a trench along the wall of a big room—no stalls or seats! In the dining room I received a tin cup and bowl and lined up for my first meal. It was rice with plums, and tasted awful! That night I tried to sleep, but it was unbearably hot and humid. Even worse were the mosquitoes, a severe problem around camps. I told myself, 'Hermann, if you want to go on living, you just have to get used to everything, no matter how hard and unpleasant things are.' "

Shanghai's streets were drab and dirty; there were ruins everywhere, but the European refugees had begun to rebuild houses, stores, restaurants, and cafés. Chusan Road came to be known as Little Vienna, with its coffeehouses and bakeries. Life started to bloom out of the ruins. At night the streets were filled with Chinese sleeping on bamboo mats on the sidewalks, because it was too hot in their houses. Every morning, city workers picked up the dead bodies wrapped in straw mats that had been put out onto the streets during the night because people had no money for proper burials. For the refugees from Europe, these things were horrible to witness.

"Illnesses also made life terrifying," Hermann says. "You could not eat raw fruits or vegetables;

Opposite page, left to right: Selig and Miriam Goldfarb with baby Hermann, Munich, 1920; Selig and Miriam with Hermann and his sister, Sonja, 1922; Hermann, age 13, Berlin, 1932.

"My mother told me to go into hiding until the action was called off. I left work immediately and stayed for two weeks with friends. Luckily I was still in hiding when Kristallnacht *occurred. It was the beginning of the horrors that would follow."*

everything had to be cooked, and water had to be boiled to prevent dysentery. Thousands of refugees were stricken, and hundreds died from it. Others caught typhus and cholera."

But there were pleasant times as well. "After crossing the Garden Bridge, where Japanese soldiers were standing guard, you were in the International Settlement," Hermann recalls. "The Broadway Mansion, a large modern building, was very impressive. The city was very different here. There was the Bund, with its beautiful buildings, fine stores, hotels, and theaters. There were interesting jetties and ships along the waterfront. And there was a beautiful park, the Shanghai Public Gardens.

"And there were also dozens of prostitutes in front of Wing On's department store, but the saddest thing was seeing mothers offering their young daughters to men."

The weather continued to be brutal—hot and humid in the summer, with temperatures often higher than 100 degrees and no relief at night. In the winter, it was cold and rainy. When a typhoon raged, the water level in the river rose dramatically, and dirty water would back up through the open sewer system into the streets, flooding them and the houses.

Despite these hardships, life in the refugee camps became more normal: Since everybody was in the same boat, a bond developed between the refugees, making life easier to bear. Schools were established; a hospital opened at the Ward Road Heim; synagogues provided services; a refugee orchestra gave concerts, and several newspapers were published.

By August 1939 the refugee population had grown to more than 18,000 people. Then Japan (a German ally) invaded China. After taking control of China, the Japanese restricted the entry of Jewish immigrants. Those seeking entry had to deposit 400 U.S. dollars in Chinese banks and register with Japanese

authorities. These measures slowed immigration to a trickle. "I was lucky that I had arrived when I did," Hermann says.

Adapting, Always Adapting

FINDING WORK SEEMED impossible, especially in Hermann's profession, cabinetmaking. The Chinese were not used to seeing a white man perform any manual labor; according to British colonial policies, they could be bosses only. So Hermann tried his luck selling things, but, he says, "I was no salesman. One day I heard of a job in a cabinet shop. It was far away—a three-hour commute each way—and offered low wages. But I took the job anyway, and rented a small room. After three weeks I had to quit, because I was exhausted. Disillusioned, I moved back into the camp. Then, in May 1940, a couple from Vienna opened a knittingwear factory. They were looking for a supervisor, and I got the job.

"In the mosquito-ridden refugee camp, I told myself, 'Hermann, if you want to go on living you just have to get used to everything, no matter how hard and unpleasant things are.'"

"That's how I met Else Ruben, a German Jew from Berlin who was working there. She lived with her mother, Betty, a widow, on Baikal Road in a house owned by her uncle. Many of her relatives from Germany were living there. Since I needed a place to live, Else invited me to stay in a small, partitioned area of the room which she and her mother shared. I was invited to have meals with them as well. The arrangement worked out beautifully.

"I worked at the knitting factory until 1941, when I heard that ORT (Organization for Rehabilitation Through Training) was opening a trade school to train adults for jobs when they resettled. I was hired to teach woodworking. My salary was $15 a month—a pretty good wage.

"Then, on December 7, 1941, Japan attacked Pearl Harbor. America declared war on Japan and American support was cut off. Local organizations took up the slack, but there was no money for teachers at ORT. They asked us to work without pay. (We were never reimbursed!)

"I continued living with Else and her mother and began doing some embroidery work at Else's factory to earn extra money. A year later, the Japanese moved all stateless refugees into a ghetto in Hongkew, a crowded area where it was hard to

Top: Postcard of *Hakozaki Maru* sent by Hermann to his mother en route to Shanghai, July, 1939.

Bottom right: Facsimile of pass that allowed refugees to leave Shanghai ghetto, issued by Japanese authorities, 1945.

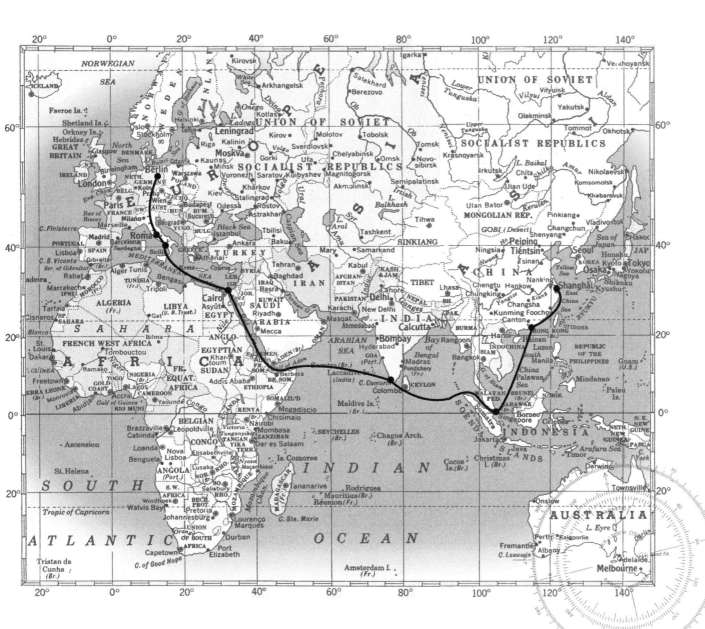

Hermann took a train from Berlin to Rome, then Naples. On July 2, 1939, he boarded a freighter bound
for China. The ship sailed to Port Said, then sailed through the Suez Canal. On July 28 the ship passed Hong Kong;
on July 31—after sailing for almost a month—Hermann finally reached Shanghai.

find housing. To help out, SACRA, a relief organization, bought some empty warehouses and remodeled the interiors, making single rooms available. Else, her mother, and I decided to apply for a room together. We got a tiny room with a bed and table; a common washroom and toilet were located in the corridor. We were not allowed to leave the ghetto under threat of severe punishment. We needed a special pass to leave. The situation there was hardly good, but we

had many friends. Our life was as pleasant as possible.

"When the war in Europe ended, in May 1945, the Japanese erected machine-gun bunkers around our ghetto. We were sure that they'd kill us if the Allies landed in Shanghai. Luckily for us, that didn't happen.

"Then the U.S. began to bomb in the Shanghai area. We hid under beds and tables, hoping the bombs would not fall near us. On July 17, 1945, bombs fell on Hongkew, and thirty-two refugees died. Many

others were wounded. Houses collapsed from the shock waves. We were fortunate to escape. The next few weeks were very tense. After the U.S. bombed Hiroshima and Nagasaki, Japan surrendered.

"We had made it!"

A New Life

HERMANN MANAGED TO FIND A JOB AS A carpenter with the U.S. Army. More lucky things occurred: The Red Cross posted notices from Jewish refugees who were looking for family survivors. Hermann found a notice from a woman named Miriam Goldfarb Medvediff from London.

"Since she was looking for her son, I thought right away it must be my mother," Hermann says. "She must have remarried. I sent her a message through the Red Cross. I received an answer. She was my mother! She had emigrated to London before the war on a domestic permit. There she had married Nachman Medvediff. My sister, Sonja, also in England, had married an Austrian refugee. My brother, Eric, was living in France; he had fought with the French Resistance. Even my Aunt Martha, who had

been sent to a labor camp in Russia, was alive. We were fortunate that so many of us had survived. We had not communicated in almost eight years.

"Else and I married and hoped to emigrate to America. In the meantime, I opened a woodworking shop with Bruno Schleich, a former pupil."

On April 30, 1947, Else gave birth to a daughter, Helen. Soon after, Else's mother left to join her brother in New York City. Then the Communist forces of Mao Tse-tung moved toward Shanghai. Hermann and Else had to depart by December 31 or their visas would expire. There was little space available on airplanes. But they packed so they would be ready.

"On December 16, 1948, at exactly 9 a.m., the telephone rang. We had to go to the airport immediately," Hermann says. "We didn't even have time to say good-bye to the family.

"We arrived in San Francisco on December 18, 1948, after flying for thirty-four hours. Eventually we settled in Rochester to be near my parents and sister, who were in Toronto. Life in Rochester was good to us. Eventually, my parents, my brother, Eric, and my Aunt Martha moved to Toronto. Our family was united again. But my aunt Helene and Fanny and Fanny's son, Heniek, were missing. They had been killed in Auschwitz.

"In 1954 we became American citizens. That was the highlight of my life. Since that time my mother and my sister passed away. In 1986, Else tragically died from cancer. The following year I began dating Senta Schlesinger, the widow of a family friend; we have decided to spend our lives together. We enjoy our families, travel a lot, and we are very happy.

"Aunt Martha is now the matriarch of our family. Eric and I are next in line. But the future belongs to my daughter, Helen; my granddaughter, Lisa Michelle; and my nieces and my nephews and their children." ✡

Top: Hermann Goldfarb and his companion, Senta Schlesinger.

Shanghai

Jews in Shanghai

right: Jewish refugees in metalshop in
gliang Road Heim. Top left: Jewish
ugees in front of their store. Bottom:
rd and Kwemming Road, where the first
mp for the poorest Jewish refugees was
ablished.

By the time that German Jews emigrated to China, there were already two Jewish communities in Shanghai. One was a small but very rich community of *Sephardi* Jews, whose ancestors had emigrated to the city in the nineteenth century from Baghdad. The other, larger, community was composed of *Ashkenazi* Jews, most of them well-off Jews from Russia. In the 1930s, more than 17,000 Jewish refugees from Germany and Austria began to arrive. Many had little money. So the local Jewish communities organized a relief committee to help them.

Help also arrived from American Jewish organizations, which established *Heime* (camps) to provide housing and kitchens to feed the newcomers. One of the first was the Ward Road *Heim*. There, families lived together in big halls with bunk beds. They hung blankets between the beds, but that did not create privacy; inevitably there were problems. To accommodate the flow of new refugees, new camps were established in Wayside Road, Alcock Road, Kichow Road, Chaoufoong Road, and Pingliang Road. They all filled up fast. Jews there managed to keep up their religion and culture by reading Yiddish poems, publishing Yiddish and Polish language newspapers, and studying with the Mir Yeshiva at the Beth Aharon Synagogue.

When the war ended in 1945, the Jewish refugees in Shanghai became "displaced persons" and were helped by the United Nations Relief and Rehabilitation Association. Most emigrated to the U.S., Canada, Israel, Australia, and New Zealand.　　　　B.L.

Underground in Hitler's Berlin:
The Story of Ellen and Erich Arndt

ADAPTED FROM *SURVIVAL IN THE SHADOWS*
BY BARBARA LOVENHEIM

When the Russians discovered the Arndt-Lewinsky-Gumpel group in
April 1945, there were seven who had survived in hiding—Dr. Arthur
Arndt; his wife, Lina; their children, Erich and Ruth; Charlotte Lewinsky
and her daughter, Ellen; and Bruno Gumpel. They are the largest known
group of German Jews to have survived the war in hiding in Berlin.

*For many years I could not conceive that there were
any German Jews who survived the Holocaust living
in Berlin. I had heard stories of Jews who were hidden by non-Jews in countries like Hungary, France,
and Czechoslovakia, but I had never heard stories of
Jewish survivors in Berlin—Hitler's headquarters—
where, I assumed, antisemitism was more virulent
than in other German cities.*

*Then I met Ellen and Erich Arndt, a gracious
couple in their mid-seventies who now live in
Brighton, a suburb of Rochester, New York. They are
a pleasant, no-nonsense couple who share a delight-
ful sense of humor, a lively intellect, and a calm, reserved demeanor. The Arndts have two daughters,*

*six grandchildren, and two great-grandchildren, all
of whom are sources of joy and activity. It is hard to
imagine that Ellen and Erich lived underground in
war-torn Berlin with five other Jews. Here is their
remarkable story, a story not only of daring and
courage, but of extraordinary human kindness.*

IN DECEMBER 1942, ERICH ARNDT PERSUADED
his father, Arthur Arndt, a successful Jewish physician, to risk living in the precarious world of the
Berlin underground rather than face the certainty of
deportation to the Nazi death camps. Erich, only 19,
was working as a slave laborer at Siemens, a gigantic

defense company. There, he had heard through the *Mundfunk*—the Jewish rumor mill—that a massive factory raid was being planned. Jewish slave laborers would be deported and Berlin would finally be *Judenrein* (free of Jews). Erich knew that he and all his loved ones—his parents; his sister, Ruth; his girlfriend, Ellen Lewinsky; and Ellen's mother, Charlotte—were vulnerable. Erich decided they had only one chance to survive: They would have to go underground and live without legal identity cards, ration cards, or even jobs, depending upon their own wits and the kindness of German non-Jews to protect them.

Before the Storm

ELLEN LEWINSKY, A BLOND TODDLER WITH gray-blue eyes, grew up in Blesen, Germany, a tiny farming village in eastern Germany, with her mother, Charlotte Gurau Lewinsky, and her grandparents, Siegfried and Henriette Gurau. Siegfried, a grain merchant, was well-liked by the townspeople, even though the Guraus were the only Jewish family in the tiny town.

When Hitler came to power in 1933, things changed for the Guraus. Ellen, only 13 and a top student, had to drop out of school. Siegfried's store was boycotted by German officials. Neighbors began spying on them. "When my grandmother died in 1935, she warned us that more and more terrible things would occur," recalls Ellen. "And she was right."

During *Kristallnacht* the 70-year-old Siegfried was arrested and put into jail. Soon he died of a stroke, and Charlotte was forced to sell the house and business to the Germans for a ridiculously low price. Then Charlotte wrote to Johanna Kroner, Siegfried's youngest sister, and told her that she and Ellen were moving to Berlin and wanted to stay with her. The isolation in Blesen was intolerable. At least in Berlin they had family and friends. And there Charlotte hoped to get an exit visa to join her brother, Heinz, who had emigrated to Brazil.

Charlotte and Ellen arrived in Berlin in May 1939. A month later an event occurred that would change—and ultimately save—their lives: At a family party, Ellen met Erich Joachim Arndt, the son of a successful Jewish physician. Erich, not quite 16, was smitten right away. "I proposed on our second date and said we would move to America and have a large Buick and two children," recalls Erich proudly. "And we did!"

The Arndts lived in Kreuzberg, a largely working-class district in southeastern Berlin, where anti-Fascist sentiment was strong. Dr. Arndt, a World War I veteran who had won an Iron Cross for outstanding service, was known as a thorough and compassionate physician: He had a large clientele of non-Jewish

Opposite page: Erich Arndt's work permit for Siemens, September 1941. This page: Erich (left) working in Max Köhler's factory while he was in hiding, 1943.

patients, and he charged those who couldn't pay his full fee only what they could afford.

But soon the Arndts became victims of repressive antisemitic laws. Dr. Arndt had to give up his Gentile patients; Erich had to drop out of the gymnasium—where he had been a top student and athlete. Ruth also had to change schools. Dr. Arndt was forced to move the family out of their spacious apartment and into a tiny, drab, noisy two-room apartment on a commercial thoroughfare. Dr. Arndt tried to get visas to America, but he couldn't. So the family resigned itself to waiting out the war in Germany.

Working as Slave Laborers

WHEN THE GERMANS BEGAN DRAFTING Jews to work as slave laborers in munitions factories, 17-year-old Erich was recruited to work at Siemens, a huge munitions factory that employed 5,000 Jewish men and women during the war. Erich, worked twelve-hour days, and also commuted four hours to and from work. Ellen worked at Firme Schubert, making parts for guns to go on German airplanes. She worked nine hours a day. Both were paid less than half of the wages that "Aryan" workers received for working only eight hours.

"We did not receive ration cards for meat, eggs, milk, or other healthful food," recalls Ellen. "We had to stand up on buses and subways and we could only shop at restricted hours every day. We worked twice as hard as Germans and received half as much money and food."

During this time the deportation of German Jews to concentration camps increased. As friends and relatives were sent away, Ellen and Erich feared that their time was running out; the factories would not protect them forever. Then, in the fall of 1942, Erich heard reports of an impending factory raid. He soon decided that they had only one chance to survive; they had to go into hiding. Ruth and Ellen agreed to go with him; they knew it was their only chance.

Into the Shadows

BUT WHEN ERICH PROPOSED THE IDEA TO his father, Dr. Arndt was thoroughly against it. "Who will protect us and feed us?" challenged Dr. Arndt. "Maybe one single man could survive underground. But not a group of six people. At least in the camps we will have shelter and food."

"In the camps we will probably die," rebutted Erich. "Maybe not right away, but soon. At least in Berlin, there are people who can help us. We will have a better chance of making it here."

Erich pressed the issue for weeks and finally presented his father with an ultimatum: "I told him that Ellen and Ruth and I would go into hiding, even if he and *Mutti* didn't. We would rather die on the streets of Berlin than starve to death in a work camp." Faced with the prospect of splitting up his family, Dr. Arndt agreed.

The next day, Dr. Arndt spoke to two of his former patients, Max and Anni Gehre, seeking their help. Dr. Arndt had cured their daughter, Inge, of diphtheria when she was a child. The Gehres were passionate anti-Fascists and indebted to Dr. Arndt. They had already sheltered the family on several evenings when rumors of a Gestapo raid had surfaced. They offered to shelter Dr. Arndt in their tiny apartment. Anni also volunteered to find hiding places and jobs for the rest of the family.

Opposite page, left to right: Charlotte Lewinsky (Ellen's mother), Blesen, 1920's; Dr. Arndt, Lina Arndt, Ruth and Erich Arndt, Berlin 1924; Dr. Arndt in World War I.

Erich presented his father with an ultimatum: "I told him that Ellen and Ruth
and I would go underground, even if he and my mother didn't. We would rather
die on the streets of Berlin than starve to death in a concentration camp."

"They were blue-collar workers, good Lutherans, who knew the difference between right and wrong," recalls Ellen fondly. "They were determined to help us, no matter how risky it was."

Anni then called Max Köhler, a pacifist and former patient of Dr. Arndt's who owned a small loft factory that manufactured spray paint brushes for artists. The factory was located several blocks away, on 20 Oranienstrasse. Max despised Hitler. He volunteered to hire Erich as a journeyman. Another neighbor, Purzel Lefebre, agreed to shelter Erich, Ruth, and their mother, Lina, in the large bedroom of her apartment. (She and her daughter, Ilse, would move into the living room.)

That December was bitterly cold. Erich was on medical leave from Siemens, and nervous that the Gestapo would pick him up. The family packed all their possessions in trunks and brown cartons and, during the last two weeks of the month, they moved them stealthily through the snow to the home of the Gehres, who had promised to take care of them. During this time Bruno Gumpel, a former schoolmate of Erich's and a co-worker from Siemens, happened by to see Erich. His mother and aunt had been deported to Auschwitz. Bruno, feeling lonely and very depressed, had decided to look up Erich. He pitched in and helped Erich move the boxes to the Gehres.

On January 9, 1943, Lina Arndt carefully sewed her family's Jewish identification cards into the seams of their winter coats. Dr. Arndt wrote a suicide note to account for their disappearance, and the family ceased to exist legally.

Several weeks later, Ellen found a hiding place for her mother, Charlotte, with Anni Harm, the wife of a German soldier, who thought that hiding Jews was the "Christian" thing to do. Ellen would join the Arndts at Purzel's.

Just in Time

ON SATURDAY, FEBRUARY 27, 1943, THE Gestapo raided factories where Jews were working and homes where their families were quietly observing the Sabbath. The coup was enormous: In one day they rounded up about 7,000 Berlin Jews. Most were deported to Auschwitz. Despite the enormity of this action, Goebbels, Hitler's Minister of Propaganda, was enraged. According to his records, they had not arrested everyone on their list. "We have failed to lay our hands on about 4,000 Jews," Goebbels wrote in his diary. "They are now wandering about Berlin without homes, are not registered with police and are naturally quite a public danger. I ordered the police, the *Wehrmacht* [the army], and the Party to do everything possible to round these Jews up as quickly as possible."

By this time Dr. Arndt was hidden safely in the Gehres' apartment, living in a tiny room. Miraculously, Dr. Arndt managed to stay in the apartment for the next two and a half years. The other members of the group were not so lucky; they had to move frequently, often not knowing until the last minute where they would wind up, fearing not only Nazi informers but Jewish informers who had been coerced by the Gestapo into betraying the hiding places of their own people.

Indeed, Germans who helped Jews were in constant danger of being exposed, tortured, and killed. Few Germans wanted to take on these risks, no matter how deeply they opposed the Reich. Yet, there were many unsung heroes who did just that. The Arndts can recall the names of more than fifty Germans who helped them, providing shelter, food, or employment. Many were extremely poor. Others, like the Gehres and Köhlers, were strong-minded middle-class Christians who despised Hitler and were deeply loyal to Dr. Arndt. They took enormous risks to protect these families and requested nothing in return.

"The Germans who helped us were the bravest people I ever met," says Ellen. "If the Gestapo had ever discovered what they were doing, they would have been hung up on lampposts or shot."

Life in the Shadows

IN THE SPRING OF 1943 THE NAZIS TOLD PURZEL they needed her bedroom for bombed out Berliners. Max Köhler said Erich could sleep in the factory. Max's son, Hans Köhler, who ran the factory with his father, helped Erich settle in and set up a warning device on the door leading into the loft.

Ellen, Ruth, and Lina hastily moved into a tiny room in the back of a local delicatessen that had one single cot. The indefatigable Anni then contacted "Tata" (Anni Schultz), the Arndts' first nanny. Tata had hidden much of Dr. Arndts' medical equipment in the ground surrounding her small country house, and she agreed to put up Lina.

Anni then conned a Nazi neighbor, Frau Liebold, who was a cleaning lady at the Berlin Opera, into hiding Ellen and Ruth in her pantry. "Anni told her we were on a secret mission for the *Führer* and we needed a place to stay during the daytime," recalls Ellen. "And she was so gullible and stupid that she believed us!" Then Frau Liebold's son, a German officer, began to visit regularly. "We knew then it was time to look for a new hideout," recalls Ellen. "We figured he could not possibly be as stupid as his mother and would soon be onto us."

So Ellen moved into the factory with Erich. "If

Opposite page: Ellen and Erich (left) and Ruth and Bruno (right), 1946, Berlin.

Photos were taken for their parents' silver wedding anniversary.

In September 1945, Ellen and Erich and Ruth and Bruno consecrated their marriages by having a double Jewish wedding in the annex to the synagogue on Kottbusser Ufer where Erich had been bar mitzvahed. It was the first Jewish wedding in Berlin after the war.

they are going to kill me for hiding one Jew, they might as well kill me for hiding two," said Max, who did not tell his wife, Klara, for fear that she would be afraid and pressure Max to move them both out. Ruth moved in with her mother at Tata's. Then Charlotte had to move, because the neighbors were becoming suspicious. Ellen found her a room with a prostitute. But the neighbors there also became suspicious.

"It seemed we were always looking for hiding places for my mother," says Ellen. "But she was incredibly good natured, and always managed to endure."

Charlotte was also extremely feisty. She had insisted on taking a fancy dress, feathered hat, and two silver-fox boas into hiding; sometimes she would brazenly put them on and take a train into the busiest section of Berlin. There she would find a restaurant packed with German officers, ask to be seated next to a high-ranking one and, before ordering from the waiter, fumble in her purse, pretending to look for

her ration stamps. *"Ach,"* she would exclaim, "I left them at home." Inevitably the officer would give her some of his cards. She would then feast on a meal of roasted goose and the trimmings, often slipping portions into her purse to share with the others!

Köhler's Factory

SOON ENOUGH KÖHLER'S FACTORY BECAME home base for everyone. Ruth would stay there from time to time. Bruno Gumpel, who had helped the Arndts move, looked up Erich and became a regular visitor. Dr. Arndt would try to visit late at night, every couple of weeks, bringing medicine and checking up on his family's health. "We did not see each other often, or even on a regular basis," recalls Ruth. "Sometimes my father would come up to the factory. Sometimes we would meet in the dark, at a prearranged street corner, where we exchanged little

Berlin 1950

Some of the Arndts' many protectors. Clockwise, from top left: Anni Gehre, who hid Dr. Arndt and organized hiding places for the others, and her grandson, Michael, 1950; Purzel Lefebre (left) and Charlotte with two German soldiers, 1943. Purzel hid four members of the group in her home. Anni Harm with her daughter, Evelyn, 1943. Anni hid Charlotte for six months. The Santaellas with their Rightous Gentile certificate in Spain. They hid Ruth and Lina Arndt for five months. The Arndts with the Düblers in 1989. Gretchen (far right) sent ration cards to the group. Ruth Gumpel with Santaellas at a picnic in the Harz Mountains, 1944. Opposite page, left: Max and Klara Köhler, 1946; right: Hans Köhler, 1943. Max and Hans hid six members of the group in their factory during the war. Klara never knew.

"If they are going to kill me for hiding one Jew, they might as well kill me for hiding two Jews," said Max Köhler. By the end of the war, Max was hiding six Jews in his factory.

bits of food or soap we had gathered. He would bring us food from the Gehres when he could, and give us medicine and vitamins."

On weekends, the group would sit around a large table, playing gin rummy and listening to the BBC on Hans Köhler's radio. And they would also intercept military reports on a wireless set up by Erich. They would take turns bathing and washing their clothing in a basin. Ellen cooked meals on a Bunsen burner. Socks were a continual problem, and Ellen—trained as a seamstress—would carefully make new soles by cutting off and using the tops of the worst of them.

"We tried to look as well-dressed and normal as possible, since we didn't want to appear conspicuous," says Ellen. "We were scared of the bombs, but we knew that the more bombs came, the more chance we would be rescued soon."

Since Ruth and Ellen had to be out of the factory by the time workers arrived, it was Ellen's job to assign jobs and make sure everyone would be accounted for. They found most jobs through word of mouth. "Help was extremely scarce," says Ellen. "People did not ask many questions. We never revealed our last names to them. We left nothing to chance."

One such employer was Herr Wehlen—a colonel in the German army who used his connections to buy goods from occupied countries and sell them for huge mark-ups on the Black Market. Herr Wehlen and his wife had few scruples—about harboring Jews or anyone else. He hired Ellen and Ruth to take care of his children, clean his house, serve his guests when they came to dine, and cook an occasional goose. They were warm and well-fed; they could also take food home to share with the others.

The following April 1944, Ruth and Lina were introduced to a Spanish diplomat, Dr. Santaella, a devout Catholic who was hiding another Jewish woman in his large home in the German countryside, right next to the Japanese consulate. He hired Ruth as a nanny for his four children; then he hired Lina as a cook. None of the servants knew that the two women were related; they would make faces at each other as they passed on the stairways.

City Under Siege

IN SEPTEMBER OF 1944 DR. SANTAELLA WAS transferred to Switzerland. Ruth and Lina had to return to Berlin, where they moved constantly, from hiding place to hiding place. "It seems I never knew

*The Arndts and Gumpels visited each other frequently through the years
and remained the best of friends, bonded together by their perilous journey through
the darkest hours of Berlin. Köhler's factory also survived the war.*

where I was going to sleep; I kept all my possessions with me in a small tote bag so I could move instantly," recalls Ruth. As bombs tore up Berlin, it became harder and harder to find refuge. Charlotte was bombed out of her hiding place; then Bruno was bombed out. They moved into the factory because they had no place else to go.

Bruno and Ellen—who looked the most "Aryan" because they were blond—would steal food and ration cards whenever possible. Bruno would sometimes trade cigarette butts for edibles and, after bombings, he stood in food lines impersonating a homeless Berliner. Ellen and her mother would sometimes ride the subway for hours and hours, when they had no place else to go. Then, early in 1945, Lina and Ruth ran out of hiding places and moved into the factory. From that time on there were six of them in Max's fac-

tory full-time: Lina and Charlotte slept on cots in a front office; Ellen and Erich slept on thin blue mattresses on the floor, and Bruno and Ruth stayed on bunk beds in a small storage room in the back.

During the day, Erich and Bruno worked side by side, posing as Gentile journeymen. Ellen sometimes worked on the floor with them, while Lina, Charlotte, and Ruth hid in the tiny, windowless storage room. There they could not talk, for fear of alerting the other factory workers. Even urinating into a pail was dangerous, since it could bring detection by the workers. (Max's wife, Klara, still didn't know they were there.)

As bombing became more intensive, they had less and less to eat. One day the vibration from an air raid near the factory shattered the factory's windows. Glass flew into a pile of noodles that Ellen had made, almost ruining their small ration of food. Then Bruno found ration cards—for 100 pounds of chicken feed. Ellen cooked them for several months.

"Then they began to walk!" recalls Ellen. "They eventually became infested with worms. I tried to remove them, but I couldn't. So I cooked them anyway and served them to everyone in the dark."

They would have starved without the feed.

Deliverance

WHEN THE RUSSIANS ARRIVED IN LATE April, Erich weighed a mere 100 pounds; Ellen and Ruth weighed only 90 pounds and the others were similarly gaunt. The Russians did not believe that they were *"Juden"* until Erich recited the *Shema* (a Hebrew prayer) to a Russian Jewish officer. The officer then brought them food and put up a sign alerting the Russian soldiers to leave them alone during the looting, raping, and pillaging that soon occurred.

On June 16, 1945, Ellen and Erich married in a registrar's office and held a wedding reception in the factory. It was attended by many of their Gentile protectors. When Ruth and Bruno planned to marry the following fall, both couples decided to have a double ceremony in the small synagogue at Kottbusser Ufer, where Erich had been bar mitzvahed. It was the first Jewish wedding ceremony to occur in Berlin after the war, and the sanctuary was filled with friends and protectors, as well as a few high government officials.

As life in Berlin normalized, Dr. Arndt returned to his medical practice and moved the family into a large, nine-room apartment that had been occupied during the war by a Nazi. In the spring of 1946, Erich and Bruno applied for entry to the U.S. under President Truman's special legislation. In May the two couples and Charlotte boarded the *Marine Flasher*, an 11,000-ton former troop carrier that was the first to transport Jewish war refugees to America. Ellen was six months pregnant at the time and one of the few people aboard who didn't become seasick. When they arrived on the docks of New York on May 20, 1946, they were met by reporters, relatives, and members of the Jewish community. Six months later, Dr. Arndt and Lina joined them in America.

Erich and Bruno both got jobs on Long Island as tool-and-die makers, a skill they had learned in Max Köhler's factory. Erich and Ellen moved to Hempstead, New York, and raised two daughters. In 1957, they moved to Rochester because Erich received a job offer as a production manager with Rochester Alliance Tool and Die Company. Dr. Arndt got a job with a nursing home in New York City, then continued his practice at the Hebrew Home for the Aged.

In 1954 Bruno was hired as a technician with CBS. Eventually he became a chief technical supervisor. He stayed there for thirty years, commuting most of the time from Queens, where he and Ruth had purchased a house and were raising two sons. Ruth, trained as a nurse, finally got a chance to work as a pediatric nurse with St. Mary's Children's Hospital. The two families visited each other frequently through the years and remained the best of friends, bonded together by their perilous journey through the darkest hours of Berlin. Several years ago Bruno and Ruth moved to California to be with their son and grandson. A couple of years later, Bruno died from cancer. Ellen, Erich, and Ruth are now the surviving members of the seven who went underground. Ruth talks with her brother and sister-in-law regularly and visits them often.

Köhler's factory on 20 Oranienstrasse also survived the war. The original building still remains (replete with remnants of an electrical wiring system that Erich had installed as a warning device). It is located less than five miles from the Reichstag. ✡

The behavior of the Vienna Nazis was worse than anything I had seen in Germany. There was an orgy of sadism. Day after day large numbers of Jewish men and women could be seen scrubbing the sidewalk and cleaning the gutters. While they worked on their hands and knees with jeering storm troopers standing over them, crowds gathered to taunt them. Hundreds of Jews, men and women, were picked off the streets and put to work cleaning public latrines and the toilets of the barracks where the SA and the SS were quartered. Tens of thousands more were jailed. Their worldly possessions were confiscated or stolen.

From *The Rise and Fall of the Third Reich*, by William Shirer, the CBS correspondent who personally witnessed the rise of Hitler and Nazism in Germany and Austria.

Anschlu

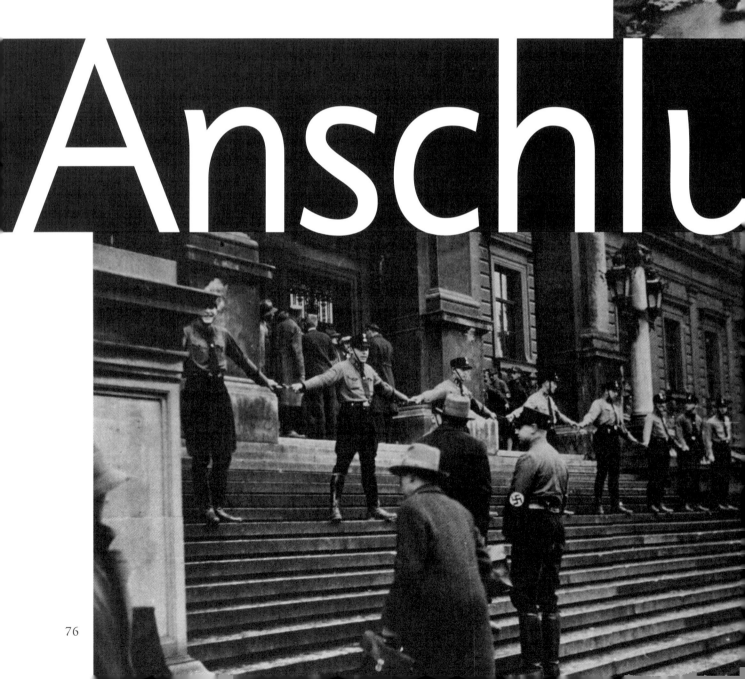

Clockwise, from left: Austrians look on as Jews are forced to scrub the pavement on their hands and knees; streetcar adorned with swastikas announces an upcoming speech by Rudolf Hess supporting the *Anschluss*; view of public building bearing Hitler's quote: "Those of the same blood belong in the same Reich!"; SA men on the steps of the University of Vienna try to prevent Jews from entering.

The *Anschluss*: Germany Annexes Austria

fter World War I ended in 1918, the Austro-Hungarian mpire was dismantled and Austria emerged as a sepa-te but weak republic. As political turmoil rocked the ew nation, the Social Democrats, a liberal party popular Vienna with the working classes, tried to restore order nd jobs. In 1929 the Great Depression set off another ave of massive unemployment. It was in these harsh mes that the right wing Christian Socialist Party gained rength, along with the National Socialist Workers Nazi) Party, many of whose members supported a nion with Germany. In May 1932 the Christian Social-t Engelbert Dollfuss became Chancellor of Austria. ollfuss outlawed the Nazi party. In response, a group

of Nazis tried to seize control of the government in July 1932. The coup failed, but Dollfuss was assassinated. He was succeeded by another Christian Democrat, Kurt von Schuschnigg, who tried—unsuccessfully—to appease the Nazis so that Austria could retain its independence. On March 11, 1938, Schuschnigg was forced to resign. The next day Nazi troops marched into Austria, greeted by thousands of enthusiastic Austrians. On March 13 Hitler announced the *Anschluss* (joining together) of Austria and Germany to jubilant crowds. With lightening speed the Austrian Jews, including some of the country's most distinguished Jewish citizens, were humiliated, brutalized, and deprived of their rights.

Profile No. 8

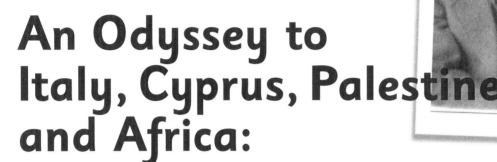

An Odyssey to Italy, Cyprus, Palestine, and Africa:

The Story of Lily and Kalman Haber

BY SHERRIE NEGREA AND RUTH HABER RIFKIN

"There were so many marriages like ours that day; it was like being on a conveyer belt," recalls Lily. "The flowers were plastic and were passed from one bride to the next. After the ceremony we just left, got on the streetcar, and went home. The Nazis were all around. We were afraid. It was very scary."

L ILY JUFFY HABER, AN ENERGETIC GRAND-mother who was raised in Vienna, Austria, still remembers the tumultuous days of the *Anschluss*. Despite reports of probable violence, Lily's boyfriend, Kalman Haber, persuaded her to go with him to the plaza to witness first-hand the Nazi seizure of power.

There Lily watched clashes between Hitler loyalists and Austrian socialists who did not want the Nazis to rule Austria. "It was very scary," recalls Lily, who was only 19 at the time. "The next day Hitler arrived and the city was filled with cheering crowds and Nazi flags and large pictures of Hitler. Most Austrians showed no resistance at all. They thought that Hitler would bring prosperity."

But Lily and Kalman knew better. They fled home for safety. Kalman, a senior leader of a Zionist youth group, knew that Zionists were especially vulnerable so he quickly burned his list of members. Lily warned her mother, Ernestine, and her brother, Alfred, to

Top: Kalman and Lily and daughter, Ruth in Nyasaland, 1943. Opposite page: Lily (right) and sister Gisela (left) in dresses made by their aunt, 1926.

stay indoors. Several days later, a young boy showed up at Lily's front door and ordered Ernestine to go outside and join many Viennese Jews who were scrubbing the streets and gutters on their hands and knees, surrounded by crowds of jeering Austrians. Most Jews, fearing for their lives, were afraid to disobey; others were bullied or beaten by Storm Troopers until they complied.

But Ernestine courageously refused. "Go tell the police or the Führer or your guard that I won't go," she said forcefully and shut the door.

Several days later, Lily's brother, Alfred, was stopped on the street by SA men. When they discovered that Alfred was Jewish, they ordered him to stand in front of a Jewish shop for the entire day, carrying a sign reading, "Don't buy at Jewish stores."

After the incident, Alfred knew he had to leave Vienna, but he didn't have time to obtain exit papers. So he joined friends who had bribed a German border guard into letting them cross into Belgium illegally. Alfred managed to find shelter on a farm near the border. Eventually he went to Brussels. There his escape tragically backfired: When the Nazis occupied Belgium in 1940, they began rounding up Jews. In 1942, Alfred was deported to Auschwitz and killed.

Vienna: A City of Contrasts

IN THE EARLY YEARS OF THE 20TH CENTURY, Vienna developed a reputation as a cultural and cosmopolitan Mecca, renowned for its wide tree-lined boulevards, wonderful strudels and coffee cakes, and magnificent concerts. People from all over Europe thronged there. Jews also emigrated there, even though the city was a hotbed of anti-semitism. By the early 1930s, almost 10 percent of the city's 2 million residents were Jewish. And under the government of Engelbert Dollfuss, a tolerant Christian-Socialist, many Jews thrived. By 1937, Jews dominated the fields of advertising, furniture-making, and newspapers; over half the country's lawyers and doctors were Jewish.

Many Austrian Jews were active in the Zionist movement, which had been popularized by a young Jewish journalist and lawyer, Theodor Herzl, who worked in Vienna. Herzl called for the creation of a national homeland for Jews as a powerful antidote to antisemitism which could erupt anytime. Young people were especially attracted to the utopian outlook and pioneering spirit of Zionism. By Lily's early teens, there were numerous Zionist youth groups in the city. Lily, idealistic and proud of her Jewish heritage, became caught up in this climate. When she was 13, she joined *Hashomer Hatzair* (the Watch Guard), a popular Zionist youth group that sponsored cultural programs, sporting events, and workshops designed to equip young people with the skills needed to develop collective communities. "The aim was to get young Jews to go to Palestine and build a new Jewish homeland," says Lily, who became a group leader. "That's what Herzl stood for."

But Zionism did more than influence Lily's philosophy. When she was 16, she met a young man there who was to change her life: Kalman Haber. Kalman, a 21-year-old engineering student , was a senior leader in *Hashomer Hatzair*. Handsome, feisty, and smart, Kalman was a natural leader, and Lily admired him right away; he shared her desire to settle in Palestine. When Lily's father died in 1935, Kalman went to the Juffys to pay a condolence call. Soon afterwards, Kalman began courting Lily.

They soon fell in love and planned to emigrate together to Palestine. The *Anschluss* accelerated their plans: As Austrian Jews became subject to the same restrictions as German Jews, Kalman and Lily decided to marry right away and go to Palestine.

But on the day that they planned to meet at City Hall to apply for a marriage license, Kalman did not show up. After waiting for more than an hour, Lily knew something was wrong: The city was teeming with SS men and Nazi Storm Troopers who were vandalizing Jewish homes and brutalizing Jews on the streets. Young men were particularly vulnerable. Lily panicked and called Kalman's home. His family told her that he had been arrested that morning, but they did not know where to find him.

Several days later Lily received a note that Kalman managed to smuggle out to her: The Gestapo had arrested him and several hundred other Jewish men, most of them prominent leaders or Zionist activists. They were being held in a makeshift prison in the basement of what was once Lily's elementary school. Kalman had volunteered to go into the school yard to help bring bundles of straw through the window for prisoners' bedding. There he had stopped a young boy walking on the street and persuaded him to carry a message to Lily.

Ten days later, Kalman was brought in for questioning. By then there were only some fifty prisoners left in the school. The others had either been released, promising to leave Austria at once, or they had been sent to Dachau, a large German internment camp for political prisoners.

Several high-ranking Nazis were in charge of the interrogation. Kalman later realized that one of his interrogators was Adolph Eichmann, the infamous Nazi. Eichmann, stationed in Vienna, was then in charge of the newly-formed "Office for Jewish Emigration," the sole Nazi agency authorized to issue exit permits to Jews. Three years later the agency was used to oversee the extermination of millions of Jews and Eichmann was still in charge. But at this point in time the Nazis were more interested in pressuring Jews to leave the country than in killing them.

Eichmann ordered Kalman to sign a document stating that he had come to the Gestapo for police protection. Kalman refused. The officers threatened to hurt him physically if he didn't sign. Kalman was smart enough to believe them. He signed the paper, saying that he was planning to emigrate to Palestine. The officers gave him fourteen days to leave Vienna.

"I need more time," protested Kalman. "I'm getting married and I need to settle family matters."

"You have to get out," they responded. "If we find you here in two weeks, you will be arrested."

When Kalman returned home, he and Lily immediately made plans to emigrate and get married. (Kalman also had to arrange for a release from the Austrian army—he had received orders to report while he was in prison!) Like many other young Jewish couples who were hastily marrying to leave Austria, Kalman and Lily arranged to have a Jewish ceremony in the Stadtempel (The City Temple) on

Left to right: Lily's father; Lily's mother, Ernestine; Lily's brother, Alfred, who initially escaped to Denmark.
There he was arrested and sent to Auschwitz.

When storm troopers ordered Lily's mother, Ernestine, to scrub streets on her hands and knees, she defiantly said, "Go tell the Führer I won't go."

June 8. But the wedding was a lonely affair, attended only by Lily's mother, Kalman's father, and two of his six siblings.

"There were so many marriages like ours that day; it was like being on a conveyer belt," recalls Lily. "The flowers were plastic and were passed from one bride to the next. After the ceremony we just left, got on the streetcar and went home. The Nazis were all around. We were afraid. It was very scary."

Everywhere an Obstacle

SHORTLY AFTER THE WEDDING KALMAN flew to Milan, Italy, to join Lily's sister, Gisela, who had gone to Milan a week before the Nazis invaded Austria to visit her aunt, Mali Waldman. Lily planned to join Kalman as soon as she obtained a visa and helped her mother close up the family's apartment. After standing in long lines, Lily managed to get a temporary passport good only for six months. Then she and Ernestine sold their belongings. But

when Lily returned to her home to turn in the key, the building superintendent grabbed Lily by the arms because Lily had left an item there, and she sent for a police officer to arrest her. Terrified, Lily punched the woman in the stomach and ran, spilling the contents of her purse as she did so. Still on the run, she picked up the items from the street and jumped onto a moving streetcar.

That evening, Lily took her mother to the train headed for Italy. Then Lily returned to Kalman's family apartment, walking through streets filled with SS men and police. Suddenly, a group of Storm Troopers accosted her and pushed her against a wall. "Why aren't you wearing your swastika emblem?" one of them asked brusquely.

"I'm not Austrian, I am Polish," said Lily, thinking quickly. Poland was not yet under Nazi rule. As a Polish citizen, Lily was not required to wear a swastika. The men had no way of knowing she was Jewish. They did not think to ask her.

Two weeks later, Lily flew to Milan to join

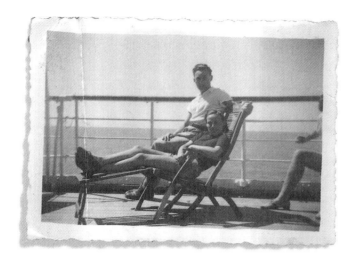

*In prison in Vienna, Kalman was questioned by four officers—one of whom was
Adolf Eichmann, an Austrian Nazi who was at the time in charge of the
Office for Jewish Emigration in Vienna. Under Eichmann the agency organized the
slaughter of millions of people, most of them Jews.*

Ernestine, Gisela, and Kalman, all of whom were now sharing Mali's large apartment. Several months later, Kalman's brother, Joseph, who had been trained as a doctor in Vienna, left Austria and joined them. In Milan he began dating Lily's sister, Gisela, whom he had met briefly in Vienna. Joseph hoped to emigrate to England as a physician. Lily and Kalman still hoped to go to Palestine. But the British, who controlled Palestine, were restricting the flow of Jews into the country. Lily and Kalman couldn't get a visa. And they didn't have much money, since they had not been allowed to take any with them out of Austria.

Late in August they set out for Switzerland where, they had heard, the Joint Distribution Committee (JDC) was helping Jews find money for travel. When they arrived in Zurich, the Swiss authorities asked them to state the purpose of their visit.

"We were just married," Kalman said, afraid to admit their real aim. "We're on our honeymoon!"

The fib backfired: When they registered at the JDC, the Swiss police were informed of their real purpose. They were arrested for entering the country under false pretenses and thrown into prison.

"I was so scared, I cried the whole night," Lily recalls. "I was in a woman's prison, with prostitutes and drunks. Kalman was in the men's prison. When he talked back to the officials, they threw him into solitary confinement." A day later they were released, but Kalman had to sign a document stating that they had entered under false pretenses. They could never return to Switzerland.

But with the money they received from the JDC, they could return to Italy and buy tickets for passage to Cyprus, a British Crown Colony and the only country that would grant them a visa. Settling there, they hoped, would make it easier to emigrate to Palestine.

They set sail for Cyprus in September 1938. In

Left to right: Lily and Kalman sailing to Cyprus; Lily and Kalman (right) in Austria with a tourist they met hiking
who was from Rochester, NY!

port, the British would not allow Lily to disembark, since her passport would expire in three months; the British would only accept passports valid for at least a year. Kalman refused to abandon Lily, until a member of the Cyprus Jewish community came aboard and persuaded him to disembark. On land, he urged, Kalman could try to find help.

"Kalman cried," Lily remembers. "He didn't want to leave me on the boat. I cried too. I was very sick. It was a nightmare."

Lily then sailed to Haifa, Palestine, where a German official took her passport and her visa. He returned with a German passport marked with a "J" for "Jew." On it he stapled her Austrian visa for Cyprus.

Meanwhile, Kalman frantically sought out officials who could help Lily. When Lily's ship returned, officials allowed her to disembark, because Kalman was already on shore. The other Jewish passengers were not so lucky; they were returned to Italy, because they did not have proper papers.

In Cyprus, Lily and Kalman made their way to the capital city, Nicosia. Kalman found an engineering job overseeing the construction of a reservoir for an irrigation system. Lily worked in a lingerie shop. They lived in a rented room; later they rented a small stucco house on farmland outside of the city. Eventually, Lily opened her own shop, designing and making custom brassieres and girdles.

They were not well-off, but they were safe: On November 9, 1938, Lily and Kalman heard an ominous radio broadcast. The Nazis were burning synagogues and raiding Jewish homes and stores in Germany and Austria. It was *Kristallnacht.*

"We were very upset," recalls Lily. "Many members of Kalman's family were still in Vienna. Soon he managed to bring two of his sisters, a brother-in-law, and a nephew to Cyprus, but his third sister and his father remained trapped in Vienna. Luckily, they got to England before the war started."

From One Sanctuary to Another

DURING THE NEXT THREE YEARS, THE Habers managed to make a life for themselves in Cyprus. Then, on June 1, 1941, the Germans drove British forces out of Crete; soon after, the Germans bombed Cyprus. All German and Austrian refugees—even Jewish refugees—were now considered "enemy aliens" by the British government. Kalman and his brother-in-law were interned in a camp with other German men.

The woman remained in Nicosia. Then the British decided to build a separate camp for Jewish refugees in Nankumba, Nyasaland (now Malawi), a British protectorate in East Central Africa. While it was being built, the British sent all Jewish refugees living in Cyprus to Tel Aviv for safekeeping.

Lily and Kalman arrived in Palestine after a treacherous voyage on seas laden with mines. But when they arrived, they were elated: They had finally achieved their dream. Even so, they were still considered "enemy aliens" and were not permitted to work. "We spent our days sightseeing," recalls Lily, "and we managed to live on a small allowance that the British provided for food and rent. But we were with our own people. It was great!"

Six months later the Habers left Palestine for Nyasaland with a hundred other Jewish refuges from Cyprus. "We were given a tiny room in a U-shaped refugee barracks," recalls Lily. "The room had dirt floors, a bed, a table, two chairs, and mosquito nets. Despite the netting, we both caught malaria!"

Nonetheless, life in Africa was relatively satisfying. Lily soon became pregnant and, nine months later, the British sent her to Zomba, where there was a European hospital. On March 1, 1943, Lily gave birth to a daughter, Ruth. "Sadly, Kalman couldn't be there for the birth," recalls Lily, "but he managed to

In Zomba the Habers moved into a small, dirt-floored stone house that was infested with with mosquitoes, scorpions, snakes, and tarantalus."You did not go out at night," recalls Lily. "You heard the lions roaring. The night watchman would keep the fires burning to keep the jungle animals away."

hitchhike to the hospital for a visit."

Eventually, Kalman was able to locate an engineering job in Zomba and they settled there. Later he found another job, managing a tea and tobacco plantation in a remote village. The family moved into a small, dirt-floored stone house that was infested with mosquitoes, scorpions, snakes, and tarantulas.

"You can imagine how scared I was," recalls Lily. "You did not go out at night. You heard the lions roaring. The night watchmen would keep fires burning to keep the jungle animals away. Besides this, there were no stores, and I had to make Kalman's shirts and Ruthie's baby clothes. When Ruthie became sick with malaria, we had to take her through dirt roads to a mission hospital miles away. She was not even two years old, but we had to leave her there alone."

The Final Journey

WHEN THE WAR IN EUROPE FINALLY ended on May 8, 1945, the Habers were legally free to leave Africa. But first they had to return to the refugee camps in Nankumba and Cyprus to be repatriated. After traveling to Nankumba, they took a train to Durban, where a ship was waiting to take them to Cyprus, They arrived in February 1946. By that time Lily was seven months pregnant with her second child and the captain wouldn't let her board, since the ship had no facilities for pregnant women. So the family remained in Durban. On May 20, 1946, Lily gave birth to their second daughter, Suzanne. The Habers finally sailed to Cyprus in September 1946.

In Cyprus, Kalman and Lily decided to emigrate to America, planning to join Lily's sister, Gisela, and Kalman's brother, Joseph, who were now married and living in Rochester, New York. Lily and her children received permission to enter the U. S. right away, but Kalman was denied a visa: Since his parents had been born in Poland, Kalman was considered a Polish citizen by the Austrian Nazi government. Due to the large influx of Polish refugees after the war, there were strict U.S. quotas limiting the entry of Polish-born refugees. Kalman couldn't get a visa. Finally, the U.S. Consul intervened and obtained permission for the entire family to enter as "displaced persons."

Before departing for the U.S., Lily and Kalman returned to Palestine to visit Kalman's sister, Mia, who had settled there and who was seriously ill. After all, it was their dream of reclaiming the promised land that had originally brought them together in Vienna. Now they wanted their two young daughters to meet Mia. She was thrilled to see her brother and his growing family one last time.

Finally, on January 4, 1947, the Habers boarded a small troop carrier, the *Marine Karp*, headed for America. They couldn't wait to rejoin their families in the U.S., but the ocean crossing was difficult and cold. Men and women were separated at night; the Habers—used to a tropical climate—had no warm clothing, and Kalman got seasick, leaving Lily alone to take care of the two young children.

These discomforts, however, were quickly forgotten when they arrived in the New York harbor. There,

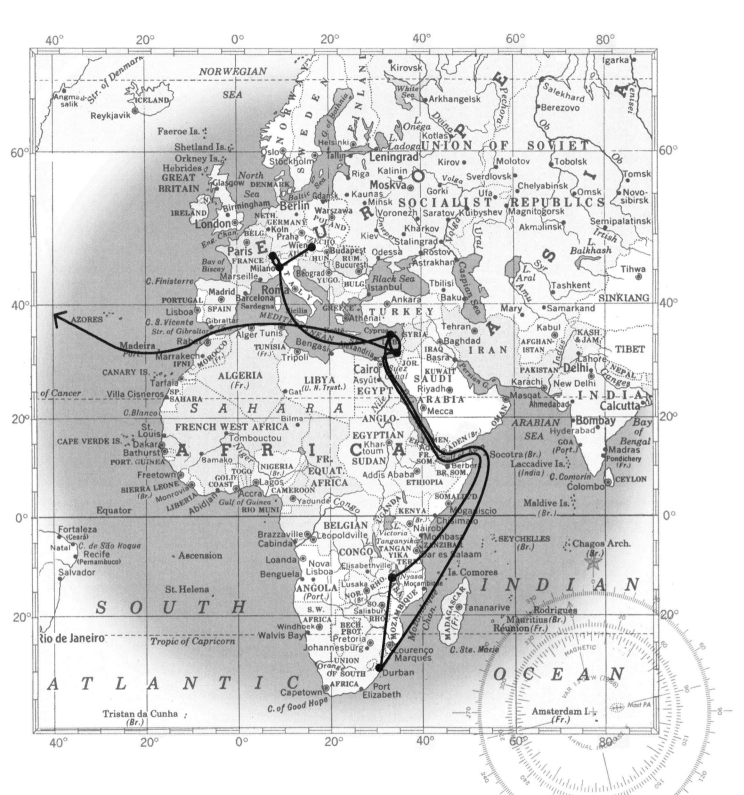

After fleeing to Milan and then Zurich, Lily and Kalman sailed to Cyprus. But Lily couldn't disembark and had to sail to Palestine to get a proper passport. They managed to settle in Nicosia, until Germany bombed Crete. The British evacuated Cyprus and sent refugees to Palestine for safe-keeping; then sent them to a refugee camp in Nyasaland (Malawi) in East Central Africa. The Habers lived in Zomba and then Milenge, a remote village, where Kalman managed a tea plantation until the war ended.

waiting for them on the dock, was Lily's sister, Gisela. The two women had not seen each other in nine years and they wept as they embraced each other. Then they all took off for Rochester. Ernestine, still living in Milan, emigrated to Rochester later that same year. Lily eventually put her corset design skills to use and got jobs helping fit women with prostheses following mastectomies. Kalman was hired by Delco Products as an engineer and he developed his own real estate properties.

Soon Lily have birth to a third daughter, Deborah. Kalman passed away in 1994. Lily is now blessed with three daughters, four grandchildren, and a great-grand son named Kalman. Her oldest daughter, Ruth, an educator, lives in Indianapolis with her husband, Robert Rifkin, a lawyer. They have two married children and a grandson.

Lily's second-oldest daughter, Suzanne, is a neuroscientist at the University of Rochester; her husband, William Thompson, is an economist. They have two children. Lily's youngest daughter, Deborah, is the founder of the Rochester Children's Theater; her husband, Michael Taylor, is a world-renowned glass artist.

This page: The Haber women surrounding Kalman. Left to right, Lily and her daughters, Ruth, Deborah, and Suzanne.

Excerpt from Kalman's letter to his grandson, Jordan, after Jordan's Bar Mitzvah on April 22, 1982.

Dear Jordie,
Could the impossible be possible? Yes it could. On your Bar Mitzvah the Haftorah from Ezekiel was read. "Our bones are dried up and our hope is lost." Ezekiel wanted to stress the point, never give up hope, as the impossible could be made possible with the help of God. When *Omi* (grandma) and I lived as Jewish refugees in the jungle of Africa, it seemed impossible that any power or country could stop the Nazis. They killed Jews by the millions and the world was silent.

I spent sleepless nights, asking, "Will the impossible be made possible? Will Judaism survive? Will my generation be living as Jews?" These thoughts came back to me sitting on the *Bimah* (altar) when you were conducting services with such perfection and devotion. You gave me the answer, because you are the living proof and evidence, that in spite of all Pharaohs, Hamans and Hitlers, *Am Yisroel Chai*—Israel did, does and will live forever. May the teaching of the Torah always guide your actions.

Shalom and Bracha (Peace and Blessings)
Your *Opa* (grandfather)

Kalman Haber's youth group, *Hashomer Hazair*. Kalman (second from right, second row from top) was a senior leader.

dealism in Progress: Zionist Youth Groups

In the late 1800's, Theodor Herzl, a young Viennese journalist and lawyer, reported on the trial of Alfred Dreyfus, a French Jewish officer who had been framed by a group of antisemitic French officers as a traitor. Alarmed by this resurgence of antisemitic sentiment in Western Europe, Herzl began writing tracts calling for the creation of a Jewish homeland that would serve as a haven for Jews around the world. Herzl devoted the rest of his life to this new mission, eventually organizing a movement known as Zionism.

Zionism grew rapidly in European communities where antisemitism was rife, appealing often to idealistic young people who were attracted by its utopian vision. Many of these youngsters found inspiration and companionship in Zionist youth groups that soon developed. *Hashomer Hatzair* (The Young Watchmen) was the largest of these youth groups. Founded in Poland just before World War I, *Hashomer Hatzair* stressed the importance of collective life, urging that in a truly equal society, everyone would work together for

the common good without receiving individual rewards. Eventually these ideals became the basis of the kibbutzim movement in Israel, leading to the formation of numerous small agricultural communities there that became the basis of its economic and social structure.

Hashomer Hatzair also spread to other European countries, where dozens of Zionist youth groups sprang up. While these groups varied in their specific orientation, all were devoted to educating young people about the need for a Jewish homeland. Most taught members about Jewish history; many sponsored hikes, bike tours, picnics, and trips. Some held agricultural workshops where youngsters could learn the skills they would need to build kibbutzim; others taught youngsters the kind of defense strategies they would need to protect themselves in a new land. Ironically, many young Zionists used these skills before arriving in Palestine, helping their brethren escape from Nazi-occupied lands and leading revolts and uprisings in the ghettos.   B.L.

profile No. 9

Interned in a Strange Land:
The Story of William Braun

BY MARK HARE

Bill Braun was lucky: He managed to escape from Nazi-dominated Vienna in 1939, when he was 18. But today, even after forty peaceful years in Rochester, New York, Dr. Braun retains this grim conviction: "As a Jew, I can never feel safe anywhere."

BILL BRAUN AND HIS BROTHER, EDWARD, were reared in an Orthodox Jewish home in the early 1920's, when Vienna was a prosperous cultural and cosmopolitan center. Their father, Max, was a salesman and bookkeeper who suffered from ill health. Their mother, Sara, was a milliner. Despite the rise of the fierce antisemitism that was to change his life, Bill still looks back with affection on the city where he was born. "I went to see all the great plays for 40 cents each," he recalls. "I had to stand through them all, but it was wonderful. We were poor, but I really did not know I was so poor. It's only when I measure what I had then against how I live now."

As a very young child, Bill experienced little, if any, antisemitism. But as the antisemitic Christian Socialists became influential, attitudes began to shift dramatically. "You could get thousands of people into the streets for Nazi rallies, even though the party was still illegal and rallies were forbidden," he recollects. "When the Nazi party established a base in Vienna, they took over a building not far from my grandmother's house. I often walked on that street. The Nazis painted the house brown and called it 'The Brown House,' because brown was the official Nazi color. I remember seeing officers wearing brown shirts as well."

By 1937, the Nazis had massive support and the

Top: Bill Braun's passport and his Belgian transit visa, 1939. Opposite page: Bill, age 2, 1923.

Nazi terror was mounting. "They were seizing Jews in the street and beating them," Bill says. "When Hitler's army marched into Vienna on March 13, 1938, almost all Austrians greeted it with great joy. They thought the redeemer had come. I was 17 years old and had never seen anything like it. The Social Democrats, who had defended human rights, collapsed in one week, one day, one moment.

"Jews lost everything," he continues. "They lost any access to law. If you got beaten up, there was nothing you could do about it. If you got robbed, there was nothing you could do about it. You had to feel lucky that they didn't drag you along."

To Escape or to Endure?

IN RESPONSE TO THE RISE OF RESTRICTIVE rules targeting Jews, Jewish organizations in Vienna opened a central soup kitchen. There they would cook hot food (usually soup with potatoes and

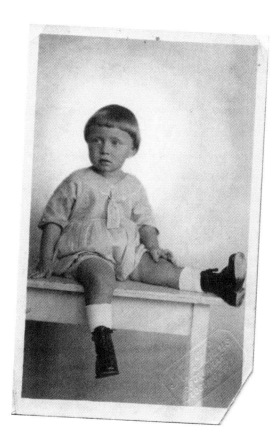

vegetables) and send it to Jews in various districts. They opened schools for Jewish children under the age of 14. (After that age, Jewish children could no longer attend school.) The Jewish community also set up adult-education workshops designed to teach Jews practical skills like carpentry, locksmithing, and radio repair work, so that if they succeeded in emigrating to a country where they didn't know the language, they would be able to earn a living.

"We lost our apartment," Bill says. "We had to move to a Jewish district. However, we were very, very fortunate. Someone knew a woman with a two-bedroom apartment who was ready to emigrate. She took us in as subtenants. My father had a small pension, and that was what we lived on. For some reason, pensions were paid.

"We lived on soup, bread, and potatoes. It's amazing what you can live on if you have to. We were forced to mark Jewish stores and apartments with brown paint. I had to write 'Jew' on the doors."

On November 9, 1938, Nazi hostility toward the Jews exploded into violence in Austria and Germany on the night of terror now known as *Kristallnacht* ("the night of broken glass"). Nazi troops swept through the streets, vandalizing businesses and burning synagogues.

"Thousands of men were rounded up and sent to concentration camps after *Kristallnacht*," Bill recalls. "But they could return, if their families guaranteed that they would leave Austria within weeks. Most men would come back with hair shorn off their head. Some had their teeth beaten in. They were so afraid that they didn't say a word. They were told, 'If you say one word, it's over.'"

After *Kristallnacht*, Austrian Jews were subject to the same restrictive laws as Jews in Germany: Austrian Jewish lawyers were barred from courts; doctors couldn't retain non-Jewish patients; businessmen had to sell their companies to "Aryans" for ridiculously low prices. Jews were forbidden to go to theaters, concerts, or films, and they had to sit on park benches marked "For Jews only."

"I don't know of anyone who broke the rules," Bill says. "Who would dare put himself in a situation where you could end up in a concentration camp?"

By early 1939, all Austrian Jews knew that to survive they had to leave their homeland. That is when Bill's older brother, Edward, who was a member of a Zionist youth organization named *Bachad*, went to Sweden on a *Kindertransport* (a children's transport) with forty other Jewish boys. While living in a children's home in the countryside, he got a job working with a farmer for two years. Most of Bill's aunts and uncles also left. Some went to Slovakia, where they wandered from village to village. But Bill's parents refused to leave. His father was too ill to travel.

Then, during the summer of 1939, Bill received a chance to go to England on a *Kindertransport*. Despite the deteriorating conditions in Vienna, Bill still felt a powerful connection to his city. He was attached to his parents and felt responsible for them, since his father was ill. "The idea of leaving was difficult," he says. "As bad as things were, I was attached to my home and my family."

Finally, after hesitating for weeks, he took his place on a *Kindertransport*. A 24-hour train ride got him to Brussels, Belgium, where he visited his uncle's family, who had fled there from Vienna. That was only the first leg of his journey to a new life. "I can still remember how I felt when I saw that the locomotives were green," he says. "In Germany they were all painted black. Those green engines—they were the surest sign of freedom."

From Brussels he took a steamer to Dover, England, and then a train to London. "I remember that

it was a very beautiful, sunny day," he says. "The boat was full of tourists. Until that time I don't know that I had ever spoken to or seen an Englishman. It was quite an experience."

An Arduous Freedom

IN LONDON, BILL WAS MET AT THE STATION BY representatives from the Jewish agency's temporary shelter. "They had a lot of experience with immigrants from Europe, but they didn't have room for us to sleep," he recalls. "So they fed us at the shelter and then took us to a place called Rowton House—a seaman's hostel—a rough place, full of unsavory characters."

By now it was obvious to the British that there was going to be a war. So they decided to send as many refugee children as possible out of London. "They found an old, abandoned castle way out in Abergele, Wales," Bill continues. "A couple hundred of us lived there with just walls—no lights, no heat,

Top, left to right: Bill, age 5, with his father, Max, and younger brother, Edward, 1926; Bill's mother, Sara, 1926; Sara's father, Hirsch Reiter, at age 70; Bill, age 22, his first photo after release from internment in Canada, 1943.

Life was strange at the Canadian refugee camp. "There was good schooling, and good food," Bill acknowledges, "but there was barbed wire all around the camp. We refugees had uniforms with red circles on the backs and red stripes on the pant legs so we'd be good targets if we tried to escape."

no water, no toilets." In spite of the deprivations, the Jewish community provided children with kosher food and a rabbi, who led them in daily prayers and helped them continue their Jewish education.

"I was one of the older children and wanted to do something useful," Bill remembers. "I knew a little about gardening, so I helped Mr. Reid, a gardener who raised flowers and vegetables. I also began to teach myself English. I tried to read the British papers as often as I could. Then I tried reading literature; I started with plays. To this day I have trouble with prepositions!"

Compounding these difficulties, Bill was not totally free in England. After the Nazis conquered the Low Countries and marched into France, fears rose among the British that they would be next. Indeed, that was Hitler's plan. Rumors spread through England that the Germans were actively smuggling traitors

and Fifth Columnists there in order to prepare for the oncoming invasion. As a protective measure, the British government began arresting people who held German passports, most of whom were Jews.

"Officers led them through the streets saying, 'Look at what we've got. We've got the Fifth Column.' Anyone over 16 was taken," Bill recalls.

Bill was classified as a "B" alien, a person whose movements were restricted by British authorities. Bill and seven other German youths were moved to a place just outside Manchester. From there they were moved to the Isle of Man, where they stayed for a month on the coast in an abandoned hotel that had barbed wire all around it, to prevent anyone from escaping. Finally, the authorities decided to ship those without family in England to Canada.

"We were sent there for 'safekeeping,' Bill says cynically. In Canada, Bill was interned at three different

"Who would dare put himself in a situation where you could end up in a concentration camp? I did not break any of the rules. I don't know of anyone who did."

camps for a period of two years, moving from one near Quebec to one in New Brunswick, and finally to an old fort on an island in the Richelieu River near Montreal. "The camp school organized by the YMCA was very important," he remembers. "We had lots of books, lectures by Jewish intellectuals who were also interned there, and even good food. Kosher meat was provided by the Canadian Jewish community.

"We were divided into two groups—one had all Jews, the other had non-Jews. I was with the Jews. There was barbed wire all around the camp. We had to wear uniforms which had red circles on the backs, and red stripes on the pant legs so we'd be good targets if we tried to escape. We tried to explain that we had no intention of escaping, that we were happy to be there."

In August 1942, Bill was able to leave camp, but as a condition of his release he had to work on a dairy farm cleaning stables. During the winter, it was bitterly cold. He no longer received any mail from his

family, and he feared the worst. After that, he worked in a steel factory in Toronto, making trusses for airplane hangars. "I was scared the trusses would come down," he recalls. "I got to know some Native Americans who were good with the trusses, because they could climb. After a year, I found myself a safe job in a uniform factory."

When the war ended, in 1945, Bill entered the University of Toronto as an undergraduate. He began tracing what had happened to his family. In Israel, he found his brother, Edward, who had emigrated there in 1941 from Sweden. Edward still lives in Israel.

Bill's parents were less fortunate. In the fall of 1940, his father, Max, died of complications from high blood pressure. Bill's aunt and uncle tried to persuade his mother, Sara, to cross the border illegally into Slovakia and join them. But Sara didn't have the courage. "She thought that because she was so good at her work, she might escape being deported," Bill recalls sadly. "And she did, for a long time. But eventually

Top, left to right: Bill's brother, Edward, at his home in Kibbuth Sde Eliyahu, Israel, 1990;
Bill with his wife, Louise (center) and their daughter, Sarah Alisa, in Rochester.

she was sent to a work camp in Riga, Latvia, where she died."

Bill's Aunt Regina died in Belgium. After her death, her husband, Solomon, and their two sons fled to southern France. From there the men walked across the Alps to Savoy, a region in Northern Italy, where they hid out with Italian partisans in the mountains. Then Solomon sent one of his sons down into the valley to find food. The boy was caught by the Germans and shipped to Auschwitz, then to Czechoslovkia, and finally to Mauthausen, a death camp in Austria. Miraculously, he managed to survive and was transported back to Germany after the war.

"It was possible for some people who had a lot of resourcefulness, courage, and luck to survive," says Bill admiringly.

After completing his undergraduate work in Toronto, Bill decided to study for a Ph.D. in German Literature. His Jewish friends thought he was crazy. "I did it for two reasons," says Bill. "One was because of the influence of a professor who was a true humanist. He was Swiss, and he made a great impression on me. The other reason is that in those days, people thought there really were two Germanys. One was the Germany of art, literature, music, culture; the other was Nazi Germany, an aberration that suppressed the humanist Germany.

"It was a very pleasant idea," he says, "but it was completely wrong. There was only one Germany. I thought I could save some of my inheritance by teaching it."

In 1953, Braun received his doctorate and accepted a teaching job at Morehouse College, in Atlanta. In 1956, the University of Rochester hired him as an assistant professor of German literature. He married Louise Zabel and they had two children. Zvi Martin, their son, is now a reporter for the *Philadelphia Inquirer*; Sarah Alisa, their daughter, is a Ph.D. candidate in English Literature at the University of Michigan. Bill, now 78, is still trying to save his inheritance. He continues to teach—part time—in the university's Department of Religion and Classics.

A Warning

IT IS IMPERATIVE NOT TO FORGET, TO PASS ON the lessons of the war and the Holocaust, Bill believes. He is now convinced that the Holocaust was not an aberration but a natural expression of German nationalism. "In Germany in the 1930's and 1940's, everything that could have gone wrong, went wrong," he points out. "Nazi power was made possible by the Germans' excessive patriotism and their habit of submission and obedience.

"Most Austrians and Germans knew that Jews were being killed in concentration camps," he maintains. "Surely, some of the soldiers who were Catholic must have confessed to their priests. But the priests never told. Even the railroad engineers must have known. They left with full trains and always came back empty.

"There are Holocaust deniers," he continues. "To those of us who went through the ordeal, these deniers are criminal. It's important that we pass on the story to the next generation, so that overwhelming testimony will show that it took place.

"The Nazis attracted leaders in every field—in art, in the army, the church, the universities. All these were professional people who could have stopped the Holocaust. But no one lifted a finger.

"From generation to generation, people must be taught. As a Jew I can never feel safe anywhere. Since it happened once, I do not think there is any way we can say it won't happen again. Just look at Rwanda, the Balkans, the Kurds, the Chinese Cultural Revolution, Pol Pot. Just look at what we do in our prisons. All I can teach my children is, you're not safe. Whether this will work, I cannot tell." ✡

Profile No. 10

A Time to Leave:
The Story of Kurt Weinbach

ADAPTED FROM *THE WEINBACHS ESCAPE*
BY PETER MARCHANT AND BARBARA APPELBAUM

Men and women who have never known persecution sometimes ask, arrogantly, "Why did the Jews endure the terror? Why didn't they get out?" Kurt Weinbach's story shows how hard it was to get out—even when you had a German general as your guardian angel.

O N MARCH 14, 1938, KURT WEINBACH, WHO was only nine and a half years old, stood fifty feet away from Adolf Hitler as he made his triumphal entry into Vienna. "He was riding in his Mercedes down Marriahilfer Strasse, the main street," recalls Kurt. "Thousands and thousands of Austrians lined the street, cheering wildly and applauding. I felt like the only Jew there, and the only person not giving the Hitler salute."

Kurt's father, Israel Weinbach, was as patriotic an Austrian as anyone in that cheering crowd. In 1908, Israel had been drafted into the Austrian army. After serving for two years, he returned to Vienna and

joined the reserves. In Vienna he was able to build his watchmaking business. But after World War I began, in the summer of 1914, Israel was recalled to active duty and sent to the Russian front. There he was made a corporal and a secretary in the army office. He also became the unit photographer.

As a reward for his photographic skill, Israel got his own room and access to a horse and cart for transportation. On trips to Vienna to buy film, he would often take photographs to the families of soldiers he knew from his unit. The families would give Israel gifts for their sons and husbands in the army—chocolates and cakes, hats, buttons, and

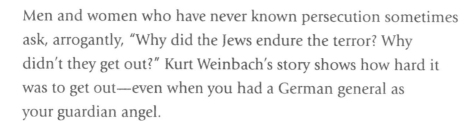

Top: Israel Weinbach (Kurt's father) in World War I, 1917. Opposite page: Heinrich Stümpfl (left), who helped the Weinbachs escape, with a junior officer, World War I.

badges for their uniforms. "My father became the darling of the unit," recalls Kurt. "More importantly, he befriended their captain, Heinrich Stümpfl. They became as friendly as possible, considering that Israel was a Jewish corporal. That friendship between my father and Stümpfl would become crucial to our family's survival."

On March 13, 1938, Germany annexed Austria. A day later the young Kurt Weinbach saw Hitler enter Vienna in triumph. His father's friend, Heinrich Stümpfl, who was by now a three-star general, was made *Stadtkommandant* (the state official) in charge of Vienna. Israel had not seen Stümpfl for twenty years, but when he learned of the appointment, he wrote General Stümpfl a congratulatory letter. "Soon afterward my father received an invitation to an audience with the general; this was, in essence, a command," recalls Kurt. "My father took me with him so that if anything happened to him, I could act as a runner and let my mother know. My father thought it very unlikely that they would arrest a nine-and-a-half-year-old."

Stümpfl had his headquarters in an elaborate Hapsburg palace reminiscent of Versailles. When Israel told the guards he wanted to see the general, they told him to get lost.

Israel insisted. "Please call the general," he said.

"Minutes later," Kurt remembers, "the guard was instructed to send my father up.

"We were shown into an enormous waiting room, all marble and gold, with statues, and paintings of the Hapsburg royalty on the walls. On velvet-covered benches sat military officers, police, Gestapo agents, high government officials, and businessmen, all waiting to be received. My father went to the receptionist, an elegantly dressed, middle-aged woman, who asked us to be seated.

"General Stümpfl soon came out," he continues. "He was an enormous man, six feet three inches tall, weighing two hundred and thirty pounds, I would guess. He was wearing a splendid green uniform with gold epaulettes, crimson lapels and buttons, crimson stripes running down the sides of his trousers, and gleaming boots."

Kurt and his father were then ushered into the general's office. "Weinbach," the officer barked gruffly, "I ought to have you shot."

Then, Kurt remembers, the general smiled and extended his hand. "All these years, we have lived in the same city and you never got in touch with me. I didn't know where you were, but you knew where I was. Now you finally remember that I exist. Thank you for your congratulations.

"Now let us talk about realities. We both know the situation. I know you're a Jew, and you know I know you're a Jew. I will do everything I can to help you, but when I tell you it's time to go, you must go."

Seven months later, on the night of November 9, 1938, *Kristallnacht*, Nazi mobs and SA men rampaged through Vienna, burning synagogues and destroying Jewish businesses. Israel's shop was spared—not because of General Stümpfl, but because Gentile neighbors stood in front of the glass windows and protected them. "The Gestapo took the keys to our business," recalls Kurt. "When the riots were over, my father went to the Gestapo and asked for them

was torn between two emotions—terror and being uplifted by the beauty of the service—which we hadn't been able to attend for the past two years. Seated in the first two rows of the synagogue were SS officers. We didn't know what was going to happen: Would they shoot the congregation? Would they set the synagogue on fire with us in it? Would they arrest us all?

"As it turned out, they did nothing. They behaved with perfect decorum. But that was the last Sabbath service held in Vienna until the war was over. That synagogue still stands in Vienna today and, unfortunately, it must be heavily guarded."

Jews Not Wanted Anywhere

BERT, KURT'S OLDER BROTHER, HAD TRIED to leave Vienna in 1938 when the antisemitic restrictions made his life intolerable. First, he tried to cross the border into Czechoslovakia, but he was caught and sent back to Vienna. Next he tried escaping to France, but he was also sent back to Vienna. Finally, he managed to get passage to China, where there were no visa requirements. He settled in Tientsin (now Tianjang), China, a city close to the capital Peiping (now Bejing), and sent his parents a letter from the Jewish Community Club in Tientsin, inviting the Weinbachs to become members. Of course this organization was only a social club—about as official as the YMCA—but the Weinbachs held on to the letter, hoping to make good use of it later.

It became harder and harder to find countries that would accept Jewish refugees. Many Jews, like the Weinbachs, were stranded in Austria and Germany. They could not practice professions like law, medicine, and university teaching. They had to live in

back. *'Raus, Jude'* [Get out, Jew] they told him.

"My father said, 'Call General Stümpfl and tell him you've confiscated the keys to my shop.'

'What does General Stümpfl care about you, you Jew?' they challenged.

'Ask him,' my father said. 'Call his office. If you won't, I will.'

The Gestapo officer threw the keys on the floor. 'Take them, damned Jew,' he said, 'and get lost.'"

The Last Shabbat

IN THE FALL OF 1939, THE WEINBACHS WERE attending a Sabbath service in the last synagogue left standing in Vienna. Located in the middle of an office complex and not visible from the street, it had escaped destruction during *Kristallnacht.* "I came with my mother," remembers Kurt. "Father didn't go with us, in case anything happened and we were arrested. I will never forget the service. The candles were lit, the rabbis were in their robes, the elders in their top hats and all the men wore their prayer shawls. I

Top, left to right: Kurt (left) with his older brother, Berthold, 1938; Weinbach family, 1930; Kurt with his parents in 1939 (taken by a *mischling* student).

"Let's talk about realities," said General Stümpfl, splendid in his green uniform with gold epaulettes and crimson lapels. "I know you're a Jew, and you know I know you're a Jew. I will do everything I can to help you, but when I say it is time to go, you must go."

ghettoized districts with heavy concentrations of Jews. Many did not even have money for food. Some Jews committed suicide, jumping from bridges, windows, and balconies; others hung themselves or sealed their windows and turned on their gas stoves.

Kurt's father managed to survive because he had a permit to run a workshop in clock-repairing for former high-level professional men who wanted to learn a trade to support themselves and their families should they manage to emigrate. In the mornings, he taught a group of Jews; in the afternoons, he taught a group of *mischlinge*—men who had one Jewish parent and one non-Jewish parent.

When the Weinbachs were forced out of their apartment by a Nazi neighbor in the spring of 1940, they moved to a one-bedroom apartment in the Jewish district that had been vacated by a cousin who had fled to Palestine. "It was small, but we managed," says Kurt. "My father lost his shop, but he supported us by running his watch-repair school from our apartment. He was one of the few Jews allowed to work."

Time to Leave

KURT'S PARENTS KEPT TRYING TO EMIGRATE, but it was difficult and terribly expensive. Finally they located relatives in the United States who were willing to sponsor them and get visas for them. By March 1940 they had the necessary documents and tickets. They planned to sail to the U.S. on a ship that left from Genoa, Italy. Unfortunately, on June 10, 1940, Italy declared war on France and Britain. Many ships traveling to the U.S. were canceled.

The following January, 1941, Israel received a message from General Stümpfl. It said, "Time to leave. Heinrich."

Their only option was China, where Kurt's brother, Bert, had now settled. "First we needed permission to travel through the Soviet Union, which was possible only by traveling first class on the Trans-Siberian Express," recalls Kurt. "It was extremely expensive, and the fare had to be paid in American dollars—

which, of course, my father did not have. Then we needed exit visas to leave Austria. But when my mother went to the Jewish Council to fill out forms, the exit visas and train tickets were waiting for her. We assumed it was General Stümpfl's doing."

Kurt's mother still had to get documents from the Russians to travel to Japan; that required permission from the Japanese to go from Vladivostok, Russia, on a ship to Kobe, Japan, and from Kobe to Tientsin, China. When she went to the Japanese Consulate and showed the invitation from the Jewish Club in Tientsin to a Japanese official, he laughed at her and said that it was useless. She asked to see the Consul General. When he refused, she stormed into the consul's office and screamed that his officials didn't recognize the letter as an entry visa because none of them understood English.

"He couldn't get rid of her," says Kurt admiringly. "Finally he gave her a transit visa good through Japan. It was enough to get the transit visa we needed from the Russians."

The night before the Weinbachs left, the Gestapo went to their apartment and checked their baggage, to make sure that they

were not taking any valuables with them, then sealed the bags.

First Class Across Russia

WHEN THE WEINBACHS boarded the train, they had only the equivalent of $72. Of that amount, $20 apiece was required for landing money in Japan; the remaining $4 apiece was all they were allowed to take out of Austria. But non-Soviets were required to travel first class, since the Soviets didn't want foreigners mixing with ordinary Russians. "So in the middle of the war, when food was very short for everyone in Europe, we were traveling in the lap of luxury," recalls Kurt. "The restaurant car had white linen tablecloths, silver utensils, and crystal goblets. We were offered champagne and caviar at every meal. The meals were very expensive—a day's food cost more than an average month's wage in the U.S.S.R. But thanks to General Stümpfl again, our meals were paid for."

At the border, Russian officials frisked everyone, looking for money, diamonds, any hidden valuables. They even searched fruit, chopping apples into slices. "Of course, they

This page, top to bottom: Professional watchmaking license; revocation of license, November 2, 1938; Authorization for classes in watch repair, October, 1940. Opposite page: Watchmaking school, Vienna, 1940. Young Kurt is standing beside his father, Israel (standing, center).

Crossing the Sea of Japan

NOW THE WEINBACHS HAD FIRST-CLASS tickets for the four-day journey by ship from Vladivostok, Russia, to Kobe, Japan. Israel exchanged them for the cheapest passage he could get—fourth class, which was below steerage—so he could get extra cash with the difference. "We traveled in the bowels of the ship, right in the stern next to the steering gear," remembers Kurt. "We were packed in like sardines. It was the worst journey I've ever made. The sea was really rough. Everyone was sick, and there was nowhere to go to be sick. Or to do anything else, for that matter. We couldn't stomach the Japanese diet of raw fish, so my father arranged for us to trade our portion of fish for an apple and a slice of bread each day."

When the Weinbachs arrived in Kobe, they spent a week in a boarding house owned and operated by the local Jewish community. Then they traveled to Shanghai, where they had to stay in a warehouse with about nine hundred people. "We slept in three tiers, with nowhere to get undressed; nowhere for privacy," recalls Kurt. "Conditions were just awful."

It became Kurt's job to get permission for his family to go to north to Tienstin and meet Bert. Though he was not yet 13, Kurt had some knowledge of English, which he used to communicate with the Chinese and Japanese. His parents spoke only German and some Russian. Since they still had no formal immigration visas, Kurt's mother showed them the letter Bert had sent her from the Jewish community center. These officials reacted as the Japanese officials had reacted in Austria. They said it was meaningless. But when they saw the "J" on the family's German passports, the Weinbach's received necessary visas.

The family managed to get passage on a ship going to Tientsin, where Bert was waiting for them on the pier. "It was Friday afternoon and getting late, and

found nothing. I asked for the slices back," says Kurt. "They were so surprised. They gave me not only the Weinbach apples but everyone else's besides. *Chutzpah* paid off."

The journey took about three weeks. "As we traveled east, through Poland and into Moscow, the countryside seemed increasingly poor," recalls Kurt. "When we stopped over in Moscow for two days, people asked us for chocolate. East of Moscow they were begging for bread."

Vladivostok, on the Russian border about three days' travel time from Japan, looked dreary and ugly. "We stayed at a horrible hotel with a group of twenty *Hasidic* [ultra-traditional] Jews and their families who hadn't eaten for days. Their *yeshiva* [religious institution] had been saved by a Japanese consul in Kovno [Kaunas], Lithuania. Chiune Sugihara, like the Swedish nobleman Raoul Wallenberg, helped many Jews escape by giving them papers.

My father, who was the leader of our group of thirteen Jews, collected all the food coupons they had not used and gave them to the starving *Hasidim*," says Kurt. "They sent out for one meal a day, which they shared amongst them. This way, they survived until they were able to get on a ship for the United States."

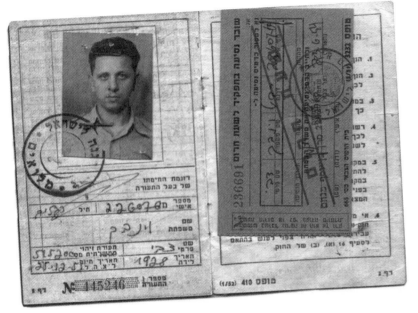

doctors, however, worked in the German-run hospital, where the Germans supplied them with medicine. There were also American marines who had been stationed there before World War II to protect American interests. But there was little social interaction between these various groups. The Jewish community, however, was so self-contained that it had its own club, synagogue, hospital, school, old-age home, and cemetery.

Kurt attended a Jewish-sponsored school with classes taught mostly in English and a Cambridge University curriculum. He learned Hebrew, English, Chinese, Russian, Japanese, and Yiddish with twenty-five students from all over the world. "I don't believe any of the teachers had teaching degrees, but they managed to give us an excellent education," says Kurt. "At our reunions held in New York City and Tel Aviv several years ago, we found that most of the surviving alumni had done remarkably well. There were many top professionals, business executives, and millionaires."

Nobody was allowed to own a short-wave radio during World War II, but the Jewish club had a legal exemption to own one and members listened to it for updates on the war. They also received wire stories from news agencies. "We knew exactly what was happening in most of the world," Kurt recalls. "We knew about Stalingrad, about Tobruk and El Alamein.

"We found out immediately about Hitler and Eva Braun's suicides in their bunker in Berlin. After the war, we found out about the mass destruction in death camps. That news came as a super shock. We

so they let them go, on the assumption that they would report to police headquarters the following Monday," Kurt recalls, chuckling.

"He didn't mention which Monday. To this day we have yet to go. Even now they could arrest me for illegal entry into China in 1941."

The local authorities then took their passports, which the Weinbachs never saw again. In the beginning, they all shared one room in a house behind the Jewish hospital, where there were about ten Jewish refugee families. Almost a year later, they found a small apartment on a side street. There, Israel could run a clock-repair business. "That's how we managed to support ourselves until the end of our stay, in March 1949," says Kurt. "My father didn't become rich, but he was able to make a living."

In Tientsin there were several different European concessions (districts controlled by a foreign country as a result of the opium war). There were British, Italian, French, and German concessions. The Jews lived for the most part in the British district. Some Jewish

They spent four days in the bowels of the ship, right in the stern next to the steering gear. "We were packed in like sardines. Everyone was sick, and there was nowhere to go to be sick—or to do anything else, for that matter," Kurt says. "It was the worst journey I've ever made."

Top: Kurt's passport to Israel, 1949.

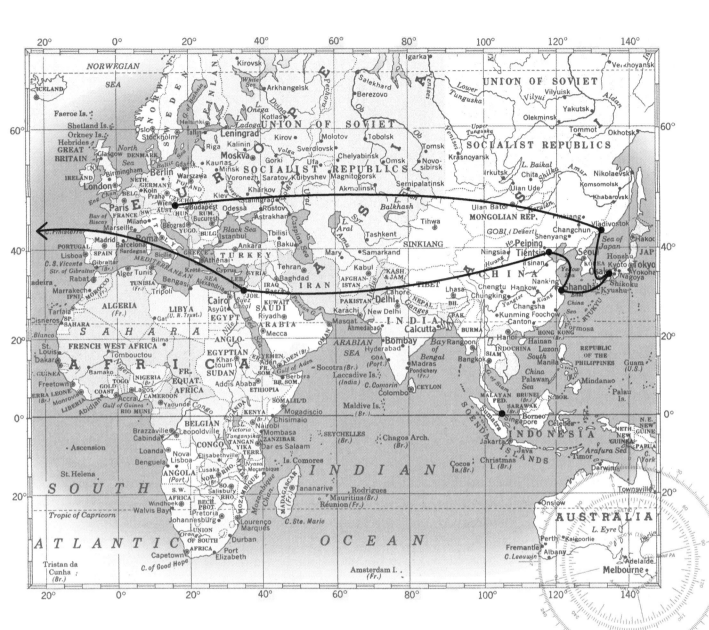

The Weinbachs traveled from Vienna by train across the Soviet Union to Vladivostok on the eastern border. From there they sailed to Kobe, Japan, then traveled to Shanghai, then they sailed north to Tientsin, where they settled. After the war, they emigrated to Israel. From Israel they emigrated to the U.S.

knew about the starvation and the lack of medicine in the concentration camps, but we didn't know about the gas ovens and crematoria.

"When we learned of Germany's capitulation in May 1945, we had to be very cautious about celebrating, since the Japanese were still in control of most of China and at war with the U.S."

When the U.S. dropped bombs on Hiroshima, killing 100,000 people, and then Nagasaki, killing 75,000 more, Kurt was away at a seaside resort and didn't hear the news. But he remembers the explosion. "I thought I saw a flash in the sky," he recalls.

"Was it the atomic bomb? My eye doctor believes I have somehow sustained damage to the retinal nerve, maybe from viewing the explosion. But there is no way to prove it."

Japan capitulated to the U.S. on August 9, 1945. Kurt remembers the streets in Tientsin filling with American troops. He saw an American officer who seemed lost and asked if he could help. "I offered to be his interpreter," he says. "He accepted. My job was to go with him to confiscate buildings. I went into office buildings, banks, stores, police stations and announced, 'In the name of the President of the U.S.A., I am commandeering this building.' I was not paid. I volunteered, because I loved doing it, being a 'big shot' and helping the Allies."

After the Communists took over China, most Jews and foreigners left. In 1949 Kurt and his parents went to Israel. Shortly after their arrival, Kurt's father, Israel, died suddenly, leaving Kurt as the sole provider for the family. Kurt's brother, Bert. married Mina Merkin, a woman he had met in Tientsin whose parents were Russian Jews. They emigrated to the U.S. and settled in Rochester, New York.

After eight years in Israel, Kurt and his mother joined Bert in Rochester. There, Kurt married a Rochester native, Sheila Gissin, and they had two children. Kurt worked as a purchasing manager for two large Rochester companies. He is now retired and is an active community volunteer.

General Stümpfl: A Righteous Gentile?

AFTER THE WAR, HEINRICH STÜMPFL—A three-star general—was tried as a Nazi war criminal and found not guilty. He returned to civilian life and died almost thirty years later. Some years ago, Kurt submitted Stümpfl's name to Yad Vashem, the Holocaust Memorial Museum in Jerusalem, asking that he be recognized as a "righteous Gentile" and that a tree be planted in his honor. "The curator told me that although there was no evidence that General Stümpfl had harmed other Jews, they could not honor him because there was no evidence that he had saved any other Jews and he may have been responsible for many Jewish losses. Therefore, Yad Vashem could not plant a tree in his name.

"Yet I know that Heinrich Stümpfl took great personal risk to help us all escape from Austria," Kurt maintains. "What he did, he did openly; he was far too high up in the German command, and far too prominent, to act secretly.

"Why did he help us? I later learned that he was a devout Catholic, a Royalist monarchist, and, I believe, he was absolutely opposed to Hitler's antisemitic policies. He was a loyal veteran of the Austrian Imperial army, and a loyal friend. By no means was he one of Hitler's willing helpers.

"Stümpfl was a good man," Kurt insists. "He saved my life and the lives of my parents." ✡

Top: Kurt Weinbach at home in Rochester.

JEWISH EMIGRATION FROM GERMANY 1933–1940

0   1,234
MILES

90,000

SEE ENLARGEMENT

ATLANTIC OCEAN

PACIFIC OCEAN

UNITED STATES

2,900

83,000

CUBA

71,100

Other Latin American Countries

EQUATOR

N

BRAZIL

BOLIVIA

CHILE

ARGENTINA

GERMANY

PALESTINE

18,000–18,000

90,000

SHANGHAI

PACIFIC OCEAN

INDIAN OCEAN

25,000

In addition, tens of thousands of Jewish refugees emigrated to other regions of the world.

1933 INTERNATIONAL BOUNDARIES

OTHER

ENGLAND   GERMANY

48,000

NETHERLANDS   30,000

BELGIUM   30,000

38,000

FRANCE

SWITZERLAND

8,000

Refuge

Flight to Safe Havens

Between 1933 and 1940 three-fifths of the Jews in Germany and Austria—some 400,000 people—managed to emigrate. More than 100,000 fled to neighboring countries—France, Belgium, and Holland—hoping eventually to return. But when Germany invaded these countries in May 1940, the Jews who had sought asylum there were again at risk. Jews who fled to Italy were also in danger when Mussolini declared war on France and Great Britain in June 1940.

Jews who fled to Great Britain, Sweden, and Switzerland fared better. Great Britain took in about 50,000 Jews; 8,000 Jews found haven in Switzerland. Others went to Sweden.

About 60,000 Jews managed to emigrate to Palestine (which was under a British mandate). Over 80,000 Jews resettled in Central and South America, especially Argentina, Brazil, and Bolivia.

An even greater number—90,000—emigrated to the U.S. Thousands more wanted to settle in the U.S. and Palestine, but they were deterred by strict quotas. In desperation, some Jews set out for distant lands, where they didn't know the language or the customs; 15,000 to 18,000 fled to Shanghai, China. Other Jews traveled to Africa, India, Australia, New Zealand, and any country that would accept them.

It was not until the war ended that the Allies discovered the magnitude of the Nazi genocide. Even so, emigration barriers remained for those Jews who had managed to survive. Only when Israel was declared a state in 1948 could large numbers of Holocaust survivors resettle there. Many Jewish survivors also emigrated to the U.S. Due to these shifts, the majority of Jews today live in large U.S. cities and in Israel.   B.L.

America the Beautiful

In May 1946, the Arndts—featured on page 66—sailed to America on the Marine Flasher, the first ship to carry Jewish refugees to the U.S. after the war. The Marine Flasher carried 800 passengers, and the crossing was extremely difficult because of choppy seas.

A MEMOIR BY ELLEN ARNDT

O N THE PIER, THE U.S. ARMY BAND PLAYS "Don't Fence Me In!" and I am standing at the railing of a small army transport in the harbor of Bremerhaven. I am leaving. Life is beginning this day, May 10, 1946. I share a petty officer's cabin with two other pregnant women. It has a shower, just for us, and everybody gets two bars of Palmolive soap! The rest of my family—my mother, husband, sister-in-law and her husband—are down in the hold, stacked three high in bunks. Everyone is excited, happy.

While we're still at anchor, supper is served. Women over 65 and mothers-to-be are in the dining room; everyone else eats army style with trays, lining up down below. God, all this food for each person! Potatoes and knackwursts, vegetables, bread and butter and oranges are on the table. I can hardly believe it. It's simply fabulous!

It's my mother's birthday. My sister-in-law Ruth and I wrap up two bars of marvelous soap and write a poem for my mother, Charlotte. She is thrilled with the gift.

At sea, I feel great and, during the day, I am with my family. My mother is busy caring for the seasick passengers, but my husband, Erich, and I sit on the uppermost deck (no chairs on an army transport)

and look at the sea—sunken ships and war debris in the channel, endless ocean past England.

A storm! I am up on deck looking down from the height of a big wave into a deep canyon of water, the spray flying over me. How wonderful, how exciting. Why, it's exhilarating, wonderful.

The crew is good to us. Seasickness is keeping many others in their bunks, so I am almost alone at breakfast. The steward tells me that I can have as many breakfasts as I want. Even so, I cannot eat like this; it is amazing to know that there is food, lots of it!

Now a funny little incident happens. One of the crew, a young man of Italian origin, hands me a piece of paper with his mother's New York address. He tells me, "In America with freedom and opportunities waiting, your husband might be overcome by it all and leave you. In such a case, go to my mother and when I return from the sea, I will marry you and take care of you and your baby!"

I assure him that this will not happen but I am touched—and very flattered—by it. After all, I am six months pregnant, and look it!

At nightfall, ten days later, we stay outside New

Above, left to right: Ruth, Bruno, Ellen (center) Erich, and Charlotte posed aboard the *Marine Flasher*. The *Marine Flasher* docking in New York Harbor, May 20, 1946, greeted by hundreds of relatives and friends.

York City's harbor. Oh, the sights! New York and New Jersey are all lit up; the thousands of moving lights are cars on the highways. Everybody is on deck until very late, just drinking it all in. In the morning, we sail by the Statue of Liberty. Cheers go up and most of us are in tears—tears of happiness.

We had bought a loaf of bread on the black market in Bremerhaven and carried it all the way into the

harbor. There, with great ceremony, we throw it in the water, knowing that we will never be hungry again.

Out on the pier, reporters. First question, five minutes after disembarking: "How do you like America?" We are laughing. Loaded onto buses. We drive through New York City. Cries of, "How big! Oh, look at the apples in front of the store! Look here, there!" We finally are brought to some of the old flea-bag hotels around Times Square.

We don't care. Plumbing only spews forth rusty water. It is not clean like our little ship. So what!

Reporters take us up to the Empire State Building. We are so dazzled, so overcome by it all that we hardly know what to look for first.

Our husbands immediately shave off their mustaches. Americans are clean shaven. They jump from the beds onto their hats. "Demolish them!" they yell, "Let's go bareheaded!" The process of assimilation has begun.

Ladies from relief agencies are there to help us. I comb my hair different—American style. A distant relative arrives with a new maternity dress, my first new dress in eight years. It's wonderful!

We walk the streets of New York, but are stopped by people stunned by our "strange appearance." We make our way uptown to Washington Heights. We have the address of family friends who emigrated from Berlin before the war began. We ring the bell, the door opens, and pandemonium breaks out. By evening, the five of us have been taken into private homes and we are buried under gifts of beautiful clothes and shoes. They do not fit me now, but I get to choose my share for later.

But now, we get into trouble with the refugee agency. We are told that we are to settle in Alabama. Well, no way! From what we know about Alabama, it is an oppressive society and, no thank you, we have had enough of that! We are not going! No help from the agency for us!

So, we go it alone. But that is another story. ✡

Photo Credits

THE RISING STORM: p. 3, Estelle Bechoefer; p. 4, *Der Stürmer;* p. 5, William Blye Collection; p. 6, National Archives; p. 7, top, Stadtarchiv Aachen, bottom, National Archives; p. 8, Lucy Gliklich Breitbart; p. 9, top, George Kadish; p. 10, Meczenstwo Walka, Zaglada Zydów w Polsce 1939-45. Poland No. 529; p. 11, VIVO Institute for Jewish Research, all courtesy of USHMM Photo Archives.

GLASER profile, all family photos courtesy of Gerry Glaser; motorcyclist, p. 13, Margaret Chelnick, courtesy USHMM Photo Archives.

NO EXIT: SS *St. Louis,* Herbert Karliner, courtesy of USHMM Photo Archives.

KRISTALLNACHT: p. 20, top left, Hauptstaatsarchiv Stuttgart; bottom, National Archives; top center, Stadtmuseum Baden Baden ; p. 21, top right, Meczenstwo Walka, Szglada Zydów w Polsce 1939-1945. Poland No. 335, all courtesy USHMM Photo Archives.

MOLSER profile, all family photos and documents courtesy of Rosemary Molser; Burning ceremonial hall at the Jewish cemetery in Graz., p.23, Dokumentationsarchiv des Oesterreichischen Widerstandes, courtesy of USHMM Photo Archives.

HEILBRONNER profile, all family photos and documents courtesy of Warren Heilbronner; Dachau after liberation, p. 34, Rosenbloom, courtesy USHMM Photo Archives.

JACOBSON profile, all family photos and documents courtesy of Evie Jacobson.

KINDERTRANSPORT: p. 38, bottom, Francis Rose; top and right, Dr. Glen Palmer, courtesy USHMM Photo Archives.

TAYLOR profile, all family photos and documents courtesy of Nathan Taylor.

HITLER YOUTH: p. 51, courtesy USHMM Photo Archives.

POLISH EXPULSION: p. 57, top right, polish riding school, Main Commission for the Prosecution of the Crimes against the Polish Nation; left, Yad Vashem, courtesy USHMM Photo Archives.

GOLDFARB profile, all family photos and documents courtesy of Hermann Goldfarb.

SHANGHAI: p. 65, top right, Yad Vashem Photo Archive; middle left, JDC Archives; bottom left, Lutz Haase.

ARNDT profile, all photos and documents courtesy of Ellen and Erich Arndt and Ruth Arndt Gumpel.

ANSCHLUSS: p. 76, bottom, National Archives; top, National Archives; p. 77, left, A.P. Berlin Collection, National Archives; right, National Archives, all courtesy USHMM Photo Archives.

BRAUN profile, all family photos and documents courtesy of Bill Braun.

HABER profile, all family photos and documents courtesy of Lily Haber.

WEINBACH, all family photos and documents courtesy of Kurt Weinbach.

REFUGE: p.103, map courtesy of USHMM

AMERICA THE BEAUTIFUL: p. 105, photo courtesy of Ellen Arndt; p. 103, VIVO Institute for Jewish Research, courtesy USHMM.